P9-DCD-678

The Amateur Gourmet

The Amateur Gourmet

How to Shop, Chop, and
Table-Hop like a Pro
(Almost)

Adam D. Roberts

BANTAM BOOKS

NEW YORK   TORONTO   LONDON   SYDNEY   AUCKLAND

THE AMATEUR GOURMET
A Bantam Book / September 2007

Published by
Bantam Dell
A Division of Random House, Inc.
New York, New York

Book design by Joseph Rutt

Bantam Books is a registered trademark of Random House, Inc.,
and the colophon is a trademark of Random House, Inc.

Library of Congress Cataloging-in-Publication Data

Roberts, Adam D.
The amateur gourmet : how to shop, chop, and table-hop like a pro
(almost) / Adam D. Roberts.
p.   cm.
ISBN 978-0-553-80497-3 (hardcover)
1. Cookery. I. Title

TX652.R634 2007
641.5—dc22
2007009737

Printed in the United States of America
Published simultaneously in Canada

www.bantamdell.com

10   9   8   7   6   5   4   3   2   1
BVG

To Craig,
the best eater I know

Contents

Introduction

Let's start with coffee cake. It's midnight and I'm stirring together flour, sugar, and eggs and toasting pine nuts and almonds in the oven. This is a fancy coffee cake—not your mother's coffee cake, unless your mother is fancy—and it's costing me serious time and money. But I am hungry for coffee cake; I am feeling spontaneous. The batter's ready and I begin to pour it into the pan. Only the batter glops out in a severely disturbing way. I recheck the recipe and gasp when I realize that I've forgotten to add 1½ sticks of cubed cold butter at the beginning. Without the butter, this coffee cake has no purpose, it has no soul. But it's too late for the butter—the window for butter has closed—and so into the trash everything must go, a graveyard of splendors that were never meant to be.

We start there, but perhaps we should start with fish: the

night that I attempt fish *en papillote* (French for "cooked in parchment"). Naturally, the recipe calls for parchment paper but I carelessly substitute waxed paper. Waxed paper and parchment paper are one and the same, I tell myself. So I place expensive fish on a square of waxed paper, then pile on the tomatoes, garlic, olives, and a generous amount of white wine. The waxed paper grows soggy, but I fear not. Soggy waxed paper is an important component of fish en papillote. As I attempt to seal my papillote, it begins to pull apart—the wine is making the waxed paper disintegrate. So I have the clever idea of using a stapler. I staple my papillote shut, place it in the oven, and wait the requisite fifteen minutes. When those fifteen minutes are up, I remove the package from the oven, cut it open, and stare down at a soggy, waxy fillet of fish that looks raw and wet and slimy, and perfect fodder for what is becoming my greatest audience: the garbage.

Do we begin here or do we begin with the pumpkin cake that calls for one cup of pumpkin, but that receives an entire can? Or the time I think dried figs are the same as fresh figs (having never seen fresh figs), rendering the Zuni Café's Chicken and Figs dish a lumpy, dumpy mess? Or should we talk about Nancy Silverton's caramel corn, the most elusive and promising caramel corn in the world—a spice-laden confection made with cinnamon, nutmeg, cloves, and a vanilla bean (a vanilla bean!), which I have ruined 18,000 times? I've ruined pans with it, I've ruined spoons with it, I've ruined furniture with it. At my funeral they will say, "He was a good man, a kind man. If only he'd mastered Nancy Silverton's caramel corn, he might have amounted to something."

This will happen to you. If you cook, I promise, this will happen. You will fail. Over and over again you will fail and then, even when you get better, you will fail some more. You will undercook your fish, you will burn your coffee cake, you will scorch, decimate, and curdle more often, at first, than you will smack your lips in delight. For those of us who come late to the kitchen, this is how we begin—we begin as miserable failures.

Collectively, then, you may ask: "Why do it? What's the point? Why not order a pizza or, I don't know, microwave one of those Uncle Ben's rice bowls? I love those Uncle Ben's rice bowls."

Listen—I understand where you're coming from. Nothing is more frustrating, more anger-inducing than laboring over a dinner that explodes in your oven, that mocks your goodwill and your hunger, that makes you never want to cook again. But here's the catch: floating above the fray is the possibility, the remote but very real possibility, that all of your efforts will collude into something joyous, something extraordinary. The smell of an almond cake baking, the sound of a lamb shank braising, the taste of your very first homemade hollandaise, are such potent sensations that no amount of failure can discourage you once you've tasted success.

Cooking is magical. Don't believe me? Pour a can of

tomatoes into a pot, add one tablespoon of butter and half an onion, turn up the heat, and half an hour later you have Marcella Hazan's basic tomato sauce. If you whisk together mustard and red wine vinegar and slowly drizzle in vegetable oil while continuing to whisk, you have emulsified vinaigrette. Remember that chemistry set you wanted as a kid? Your kitchen *is* that chemistry set, only the results are *edible*.

Cooking is communal. Nothing beats the feeling you get when you make something delicious, feed it to someone else, and listen to him or her groan with pleasure. Cook with someone else and experience the joy of shared accomplishment: an evening of Trivial Pursuit ends in bruised egos; an evening of soufflé making ends in soufflé. The choice is yours.

Cooking allows you to tap into history and other cultures. Want to experience life on the American prairie circa 1833? Make Vinegar Pie. Ever wonder what Africans do with lamb? Try Kadjemoula. Purchase a jar of curry and experience India. Gather olives, lemons, and feta and find yourself on a Greek odyssey. Coat yourself, your kitchen, and loved ones in butter and enjoy the phenomenon known as France.

Finally, the patience and passion required to cook inform other areas of your life. As you'll learn in the final chapter, my life completely changed when I started to cook. Small-picture wise, cooking is like yoga. Slicing a carrot, peeling a cucumber, whacking a rolling pin on a frozen block of dough can all be incredibly calming. Big-picture wise, cooking creeps into your life in unexpected ways. My life is nowhere near the same now that I cook for myself, and I'd never want it to go back.

The issue goes beyond cooking. Most young people (and not-so-young people) are still eating at the so-called "kiddie table"—never venturing into the world of fine cuisine and the meaningful food experience. Mechanisms are in place to keep us away from the grown-ups: financial hurdles, snobby maître d's, lack of information. I'm here to demystify it all for you and get you on your way.

This book will help you dive headfirst into the world of food, from the market to the kitchen to the dining room. Instead of a dry step-by-step primer on sauces, stocks, and soufflés, this book will bring the culinary experience to life. I share with you the people, places, language, smells, techniques, stories, and strategies that make shopping, cooking, and dining such vital parts of our everyday existence.

We'll start with spaghetti; venture forth to the farmer's market; free our mouths with olives, coffee, and cheese; cross cultures with a Korean lesbian; get knife lessons at the Union Square Café; help a former Mormon cook for his strictly religious date; face the scrutiny of my highly fussy family with a risky family dinner (including strawberry shortcake); eat lunch with a food icon (perhaps the most famous food writer alive today); dine alone at the poshest Paris eatery; and, finally, cook a tremendous feast for ten of my closest friends.

In these pages, I hope to transmit to you the spirit of good eating and good living. That last phrase—"good

living"—is a bit saccharine in this age of glossy food magazines and waxy television hosts. But I hope that through
my own, personal food story—my food awakening—you
will understand how the smallest things in life (read: the
food you eat) can help shape the biggest things, namely
who you are as a person.

"Damn, that's heavy. Did you say there'd be cake?"

Yes.

"And Asian lesbians?"

Yes.

"Awesome. When do we start?"

We start right now! All you need is a big appetite and an
open mind. Climb aboard, hungry reader: the journey
starts here.

ONE

Start with Spaghetti

The story goes that Mom, recently married, prepared a spaghetti dinner for Dad to enjoy upon coming home from work. According to her, she spent the day shopping for ingredients, rolling the meatballs, simmering the sauce. Dad, an ambitious young dentist, spent the day drilling holes in people's mouths and wiping saliva off their chins. He came home very hungry.

I suppose Mom welcomed him home with open arms and then declared that there was a feast to be had on the kitchen table: spaghetti and meatballs. Come, darling, have a seat.

If one were to observe my father at any meal—including the meals he enjoys to this day—one might make the false assumption that he was raised in abject poverty, one of thirteen siblings who all had to fight for small slivers of government cheese at a table made of cardboard boxes. And while he didn't grow up at the Waldorf Astoria, his Brooklyn childhood provides little evidence to justify the furious way he scarfs down food.

"How is it, honey?" asked Mom. "I worked all day on it."

"Good," said Dad, scarfing and slurping.

"Do you like the sauce? I used special tomatoes."

"It's good," said Dad, halfway done at fourteen seconds.

"Do you want cheese on it? Or maybe some bread with it?"

"No, thanks, it's fine. Very good. Thank you."

Were we to counsel Mom at this moment in her life, sitting on her shoulder like a good guardian angel, we might suggest that she stop asking questions now. "I think he likes it," we'd say. "You can quit pestering him."

Mom, however, had no sage marital guru—no Dr. Phil flapping around her cranium—so she persisted.

"Do you like the way the sauce clings to the spaghetti? Do you like the way the onions are translucent? Do you like how the tines of the fork spell out ITALY?"

There are no witnesses to corroborate what happened next, but according to my mother, Dad took a fistful of spaghetti and flung it at her, streaking her overeager face with tomato sauce. My dad is not a violent person, so the mere act must have surprised him as much as it surprised her. Anticipating fireworks, he fled to the bathroom, locked the door, and quivered, terrified of what Mom— already a tempestuous spirit—might do.

But Mom didn't chase him into the bathroom. She

didn't put cyanide in his toothpaste or slash the tires on his car. Mom didn't even curse his name as she wiped the translucent onions off her eyebrows. She simply chose the best revenge she could—a revenge worthy of Clytemnestra. As Dad came home from work day after day, exhausted and emaciated, Mom would greet him at the door with a warm welcome and then snatch away his car keys.

"What's for dinner, honey?" Dad would ask.

"Depends," Mom would say.

"Depends on what?"

"It depends," said Mom, halfway out the door, "on where we're going."

You see, Mom, with little exception, never cooked for him again.

If Mom's culinary career ended with spaghetti, mine began where hers lefts off. Two and a half decades later, in the kitchen of my one-bedroom Atlanta apartment, I made—for the very first time—a sauce that's become a staple in my repertoire. It's the sauce that made me fall in love with cooking, a simple assemblage of ingredients that within thirty minutes becomes something entirely new. Upon tasting the concoction, I had all the enthusiasm of my young mother and no one there to throw it, quite literally, back in my face. The recipe comes from chef Mario Batali's *Babbo Cookbook* and that's where our adventure begins.

Basic Tomato Sauce
From *The Babbo Cookbook*

Makes 4 cups

1/4 cup extra-virgin olive oil
1 Spanish onion, finely diced
4 garlic cloves, peeled and thinly sliced
3 tablespoons chopped fresh thyme, or 1
   tablespoon dried
1/2 medium carrot, finely shredded
2 28-ounce cans peeled whole tomatoes
Kosher salt

In a 3-quart saucepan, heat the olive oil over medium heat. Add the onion and garlic and cook until soft and light golden brown, 8 to 10 minutes. Add the thyme and carrot and cook for 5 minutes more, or until the carrot is quite soft. With your hands, crush the tomatoes and add them with their juices. Bring to a boil, stirring often, and then lower the heat and simmer for 30 minutes, or until the sauce is as thick as hot cereal. Season with salt and serve. This sauce keeps for 1 week in the refrigerator or for up to 6 months in the freezer.

"Okay, I'm at Whole Foods," says Lauren. "And I can't find a Spanish onion."

I have requested that Lauren, my friend and former roommate who now lives in Washington, D.C., make tomato sauce along with me over the phone. The point of this project is to prove that making tomato sauce is so easy and so pleasurable that even a self-confessed noncook (Lauren) can make magic in her kitchen.

"I see yellow onions and I see white onions," she says. "But I don't see Spanish onions. What's a Spanish onion?"

Earlier in the day, I sent Lauren the ingredients from the *Babbo Cookbook* recipe. I didn't send her the recipe itself—I was going to take her through it step-by-step. The ingredients, I figured, she could get on her own without any trouble.

Flash forward to Lauren at Whole Foods stuck in the onion section needing my help. When I'd gone to the Whole Foods in my neighborhood earlier in the day, there was a clearly labeled stack of Spanish onions. I assume the one in D.C. is the same, so I ask Lauren: "Do you see the labels above the onions? Does one of them say Spanish onions?"

She pauses and says: "I'm not an idiot! If it said Spanish onions I would've just taken one and I wouldn't have called."

What Lauren is expressing here is the anxiety we all experience the first time we shop for a recipe. "Lauren," I say calmly, "a Spanish onion is larger and sweeter than a yellow onion, but a yellow onion will work fine."

A pause and then, "Okay, got it. I'll call you if I get stuck again."

Tomato sauce represents everything I like about cooking. First of all, I like the infinite variations on a theme—if you simmer tomatoes in a pot for thirty minutes you'll have a sauce. You can make that sauce with butter or olive oil or pork fat; you can make it with onions or garlic or shallots; you can make it with fresh tomatoes or canned tomatoes; you can use fresh basil and thyme or dried basil and thyme or any combination thereof. In my cookbook collection alone there are at least thirty recipes for tomato sauce.

Second, making tomato sauce rewards attention to detail. The more you make it, the better you'll get at it. The first time you might, say, add the garlic too soon and it may turn too brown; next time you'll know to add it a little while after the onion. You'll discover that squeezing the tomatoes submerged in their own liquid will prevent you from squirting yourself in the eye. You'll know precisely when the sauce is done and how much salt to add.

Finally, making tomato sauce is like meditating Italian style: you stand there over the stove, stirring softly and fanning the smells toward your face, and you feel a deep sense of inner peace. That is, until the phone rings.

"Okay," says Lauren. "I have my ingredients. I have water boiling for the pasta. Now tell me: how do I chop an onion?"

You'll discover as you cook more and more that the

tasks you once found difficult you now take for granted. Lauren's inexperience reminds me of where I was just three years ago. Chopping an onion is one of the easiest things to do and should be a cinch to explain over the phone.

"Take your onion," I say. "Put it on the cutting board and cut the top and bottom off."

I wait to hear the appropriate chopping sounds and when I do I say, "Okay, good. Now then, I want you to cut the onion in half, north to south."

"North to south?" asks Lauren. "What does that mean?"

"It means," I explain, "you should cut it through the root end."

"Through the root end," she repeats and I wait again for another noise, hear it, and congratulate her.

"Very good," I say. "Now peel the skin off."

Crinkly noises echo over the line and then Lauren says, "Done."

"Now," I press on, "place the onion cut-side down on the cutting board with the root end pointing away from you. Make slits in the onion east to west, parallel to the lines in the onion toward the root end without cutting all the way through."

Another pause and then: "Huh?"

I take a deep breath. "Look at your hand, okay? Point your fingers at your face. You want to make slits in the onion the way there are lines between your fingers, not cutting all the way through to the knuckles but cutting all the way down between the spaces in your fingers. Got it?"

"I think so," says Lauren and I hear the knife hit the board several times.

"Excellent," I say. "And now we're going to make cuts along the z-axis. You remember the z-axis from algebra?"

Silence.

"Okay, imagine a globe. There are the longitudinal lines and latitudinal lines. You just made cuts along the longitudinal lines, eventually you'll make cuts on the latitudinal lines, but right now you're going to make cuts into the globe."

"Into the globe?"

Lauren sounds tired.

"Let me put it another way. The onion is flat on the board now, right?"

"Right."

"Turn it so the slit end is facing the right and the root end is to your left. You are going to glide your knife, parallel to the board, into the onion at the slit end about half an inch up and then half an inch higher, and that's it. It's just two cuts."

A pause and then, "Okay, I made the cuts." Did she make the cuts? I didn't hear any noise.

"Very well," I conclude. "Now slice the onion north-south with the slit end facing to the right."

"Like a paper cutter," suggests Lauren.

"Yes, like a paper cutter."

Another pause, loud cutting noises, and then: "Hey, it's falling into little pieces! I'm dicing an onion!"

• • •

When it comes to cooking, techniques matter more than recipes. It's like playing the piano: knowing one song may impress your friends and neighbors for a brief spell at parties, but it won't get you a job as an accompanist for an opera diva. When she puts down the sheet music for "Queen of the Night" and expects you to play, you can't stammer and sweat and say: "But I only know 'Puff the Magic Dragon.' "

We start with tomato sauce because it's as much about technique as it's about anything else. You have to chop the onion, you have to mince the garlic, you have to squeeze the tomatoes, you have to control the heat, and you have to salt it properly.

"Okay," I tell Lauren, who, after long discussions about peeling, smashing, and chopping garlic, and squeezing tomatoes properly, seems to be at her wit's end. "Now let's start our sauce."

"It's 9:15," cries Lauren. "I haven't eaten since lunch."

"Don't worry," I say. "Now that everything's chopped and ready to go, you have your mise in place—"

"Meez en *plahs*," she corrects. Lauren speaks French. The phrase *mise en place* translates literally to "setting in place."

"Well, now that you have your *meez en plahs*," I continue, "all you have to do is add it to the heat."

And for the most part that's true. She adds the olive oil,

then the onion, then the garlic, and cooks them for ten minutes. She adds the thyme (she loves the smell of thyme, she's discovered) and the carrot and then, finally, the tomatoes. She brings it to a boil then lowers the heat, as instructed.

"Now," I say, "let it simmer for thirty minutes."

I can hear her stomach growl in response.

"In the meantime, let's cook our pasta."

Cooking pasta is as much an art as making sauce. There's nothing worse, in my opinion, than overcooked pasta. To get that perfect al dente texture you have to add the pasta to rapidly boiling, salted water, preferably in a large pot.

"I don't have a large pot," pleads Lauren, who, as you'll remember, started boiling water an hour earlier when we started. That water has since evaporated.

"Fine," I say. "Just use the pot you were using."

Once her water is at a rapid boil, I have her add salt and then half a box of fusilli (it holds the sauce best).

"Now stir it around so it doesn't stick."

Pause.

"How's that sauce looking?"

"It looks good," she says.

"How's the texture? Does it look like oatmeal? Mario Batali says it should look like oatmeal."

"It doesn't look like oatmeal yet."

"How long has it been?"

"Twenty-five minutes," she reports.

"Now we should salt it. Take a handful of kosher salt and sprinkle it over the top to start. Stir it around and taste." When you add salt at the beginning it contributes to the breaking down of the tomatoes; when you add it at the end it flavors the sauce but allows the tomatoes to retain their texture. So if you want a more broken-down sauce, add salt at the start; if you want a chunky sauce like I do, add it at the end.

She adds the salt and says it tastes good.

"Good or properly seasoned? The mark of a great chef is how well they salt their food. I think you need more salt—add another sprinkling."

A pause and then I continue with my line of questioning. "How long has your pasta been cooking? Seven minutes? Take a piece of pasta out and taste it. Is it super al dente? That's how you avoid overcooking your pasta."

Lauren tastes and reports that it's almost cooked through.

"Perfect!" I cheer. "Drain that in the sink, but don't rinse it!"

I hear the swish of water.

"Rinsing your pasta is a big no-no—it washes away all the starch that will help the sauce to stick. Now we're going to add the almost cooked pasta to the sauce and let it finish cooking in there." I learned this technique from Mario Batali on TV. "But first go back to the sauce. Taste it. If you taste the salt, there's too much of it, but if you don't taste it and all the flavors taste bright and lively, then it's perfectly seasoned. Are you tasting mostly tomatoes or are you tasting mostly garlic? Do you think it needs red pepper flakes?"

"Ahhhh!" she screams. "I am a starving woman. I am adding this pasta to the sauce and I am eating it and I don't care how much salt there is, how much sauce there is, I'm just eating it and you're going to leave me alone. Don't call me back!"

She hangs up the phone and even though she's two hundred miles away, I can feel flung tomato sauce gliding down my forehead.

The next day I wake up plagued with guilt. Did I, with my ever-expanding enthusiasm for food and cooking, smother the seeds of enthusiasm that might have sprouted for Lauren? At these early stages of cooking, one needs to be nurtured, not badgered. I know that it's all very confusing at first. Why did I bully her so much? Couldn't I have made it easier, more inviting, more pleasurable? I've basically ensured for Lauren a future of canned peas and frozen meat loaf.

Yet, it's a testament to her good character that the next day she writes me an e-mail, apologizes for her outburst, and goes on to say: "The sauce did taste homemade—not like my usual can of tomato sauce—and the pasta really was cooked perfectly. The one drawback to the whole event was learning how to cut the onion. Man, that took *such* a long time. I wish the prep part went quicker.

Although I really did enjoy peeling the leaves off the thyme because it smelled sooo good."

Thyme is an herb that intoxicates before and after you use it. It's a powerful smell, a haunting smell, the kind that you don't smell in the frozen food aisle or at your local fast-food joint. The fact that Lauren mentions this smell in her e-mail suggests to me that I haven't failed completely, that she may have been bitten by the same bug that bit me just a few years earlier. Once you've done it, nothing can replace the sensual experience of adding fresh thyme to a pot of simmering tomatoes, onion, and garlic. We start with tomato sauce because of the sense memories it creates; these sense memories are formative. You will build on them, you will expand upon them, but you will always go back to them. A few small steps in your kitchen and the spell is cast, the transformation begins.

And what is cooking about if not transformation? It's a process that allows us to change the raw to the cooked, the bland to the seasoned, the boring to the beautiful. Cooks can take minimal ingredients and create a feast, or take ingredients for a feast and make a small tasting menu. Learning how to cook is learning to be a sorcerer; sorcerers make transformations happen. And there in her kitchen, Lauren shook her magic wand of a wooden spoon and transformed herself. It took only garlic, tomatoes, and a badgering friend.

Sure enough, a few weeks later, Lauren calls me early in the afternoon because she wants to make chicken soup from scratch. "Which recipe should I use?" she asks. "Do you have any recommendations?"

I have plenty but I'm too busy admiring my handiwork.

"Lauren!" I say. "Do you hear yourself? You're going to make chicken soup from scratch!"

There's a pause and then she says, "Well, don't get too excited. I'm just doing it because I'm sick."

But these words have no effect on me. I am elated—the formula worked. Lauren survived her sauce making without the scars that mark so many of our early cooking experiences. She is a new Lauren, a fearless Lauren, no longer the kitchen skeptic that I once knew. She started with spaghetti and now she's a cook.

Master the Market

Amanda Hesser of the *New York Times* calls me at 7 p.m. on a Wednesday night.

"Hi, Adam. This is Amanda Hesser."

"Oh, hi!" I stammer and quickly turn off the *Golden Girls* episode where Dorothy falls in love with Leslie Nielsen. I grab a pen and paper and sit on my couch. "How are you? Thank you so much for calling. This is so nice of you."

I am in a rut. I've been trying to unlock the mysteries of food shopping for a week now and I can't get a grasp on it. With tomato sauce behind us, I want to educate you, the reader, on how to food shop like a professional: to walk into your local grocery store with the cool gaze of a Clint Eastwood or a Janet Reno. Yet, each time I make an attempt my evil twin bursts out of my cranium and yells:

"You hypocrite! You know as much about food shopping as I know about macramé!" My evil twin has a point: when it comes to food shopping, I know very little. And my evil twin is terrible at macramé.

Yet, when I consider it, I do know at least one thing about food shopping. For the large majority of modern chefs who go food shopping the guiding principle is fresh, seasonal produce. This usually involves a farmer's market of some sorts. In fact, I began my food-shopping education a week earlier at the Union Square farmer's market, where I went to scout out chefs who, in turn, were scouting out fresh, seasonal produce.

And it was there, at the Union Square farmer's market, that I observed something most unusual: a woman in a floral skirt and army boots, with sunglasses on her head, standing at a berry stand studying berries. She was face-to-face with the stand's proprietor, a small Asian man in a T-shirt. The woman took a carton of berries and tasted one. I saw her shake her head no. She tried another one and shook her head again. The Asian man tasted one too and shrugged his shoulders. The woman walked away.

This exchange astounded me. What was going on here? Was this what real chefs did? Should I be out tasting berries? Was this woman a crackpot? Why wasn't the Asian man mad? What was wrong with the berries? Are army boots still in fashion? I needed help. Which is why I contacted Amanda Hesser.

Ms. Hesser, you see, spent a year as a cook in a château

in Burgundy working alongside the château's gardener, Monsieur Milbert. Her chronicle of this experience is in her book *The Cook and the Gardener,* which someone recently gave me as a gift. Since she's now a New York resident (and has been for some time), I figured Amanda would be the perfect adviser when it came to how aspiring foodies should go about food shopping in non-château-like environments. So I e-mailed her, thinking she wouldn't write me back. She did write me back and said we should talk on the phone. Which is how it came to be that she called me on a Wednesday night.

"So how can I help you?" she asks in a pleasant, eager voice.

How can she help me? Well. I begin by explaining that this chapter's meant to serve as a guide for amateur cooks who want to improve or expand their horizons when it comes to food shopping, to quit using convenience as the primary motivation for where they buy their food.

"Mmmhmm."

And yet, I continue, I realize that for most people—myself included—breaking out of a routine is difficult because, in many ways, it's all we know, and you can't suddenly become an expert on zucchini overnight or know a fresh head of garlic from an old one.

"Okay."

And with these limitations in place and with technology growing more and more efficient, our relationship with the land is increasingly compromised, and for someone like me who grew up in a world of mass-market supermarket chains and prepackaged food, going to a farmer's market can be a very scary thing.

"Why don't you ask me a question?" she suggests.

"Well," I sigh. "Where does one begin?"

I begin—as I've mentioned—a week earlier, by scouting out the Union Square farmer's market at eight on a Monday morning.

Even though I've lived in New York for a year, this is only my third or fourth time at the market, and definitely the first time I've been here early in the morning. At 8 a.m. the sky is a hazy orange and the stands are still being set up. Puddles indicate rain from the night before and there's a moistness in the air, an energy that lends everything a sense of enchantment. I buy a muffin from a muffin man and apple cider from an apple cider man and begin my studies.

I observe a man in a pink-and-white-striped shirt scrutinizing apricots. His tortoiseshell glasses make him look a little like the famous French chef Alain Ducasse, but I find it hard to believe that Alain is apricot shopping all by himself at eight in the morning. Whoever he is, I watch him studiously lean over the apricot pyramid and select a pinkish-orange specimen, which he then lifts to his nose. He sniffs and puts the apricot down. He does this a few more times and then loads a few into a plastic bag. Before I can work up the courage to ask him a question, he swiftly pays and leaves the stand.

What did I just observe?
Let's make a list.

1. Alain Ducasse sees apricot stand

2. Leans over it

3. Studies apricot with his eyes

4. Lifts apricot and feels it with his hand

5. Smells apricot with his nose

6. Buys or rejects apricot

Is this behavior indicative of a master chef or something most of us do anyway?

Let me tell you how I would buy an apricot. First of all, I wouldn't buy an apricot unless I had a specific reason to. The only reason I would buy an apricot is if I had a recipe involving it. I'm a recipe man—I buy things that someone else tells me how to use. When facing a pile of apricots, I begin by lifting an apricot and feeling its skin. If it's too mushy I reject it; if it's broken or bruised I reject it. Rarely do I smell it. Probably the apricots I pick are less superior than the ones a master chef, such as Alain Ducasse, might pick from the same bunch. I'm usually in a hurry. Will the apricots I choose ruin the recipe I have in mind? Probably not. But are they the best possible? Very doubtful.

Part of what makes an accomplished cook more likely to choose the best apricots is that an accomplished cook doesn't go with a preconceived idea of buying apricots. The accomplished cook goes to see what looks good and builds from there. If the apricots look good, then apricot tart or apricot soup is on the menu. And that's what separates my shopping style from that of Alain Ducasse or Thomas Keller (of The French Laundry) or, as we'll soon learn, Amanda Hesser. It's what marriage counselors might call the caveman theory. When I go food shopping, I know what I need before I go, and I arrive at the store with a list that tells me what I need. I proceed to track it down and I usually do so in a hurry. This makes me a *hunter*. Great chefs, on the other hand, are most often *gatherers*. They don't home in on a target—they let the target home in on them.

Most amateur cooks—in fact, most Americans, I'd wager—are hunters when they go food shopping. They go with a list. And if they can't find what's on the list, the store has little indices on the shopping cart and sometimes on the wall that tell you where to find whatever it is you're hunting for. Apples: aisle 6. Sugar: aisle 3. Tofu: aisle 12.

Food hunting is my game and probably yours too. So browsing at the farmer's market at 8 a.m. on a Monday leaves me a bit restless and uncertain. What should I be doing? I have no idea. Which is what leads me, when I get home empty-handed, to e-mail Amanda Hesser. What am I doing wrong? How does one go food shopping without a list?

• • •

Amanda Hesser's mother never went food shopping with a list. "I'd ask her what we were going to buy," says Amanda, "and she'd say, 'I'm going to see what looks good.' " Food shopping was a long, drawn-out process and young Amanda was impatient. There were no trips down the snack food aisle: Amanda's mother bought flour and butter and made everything from scratch. As for meat, Amanda's mother used a German butcher, which required a long journey by car. In other words, Amanda's childhood couldn't have been more different from my childhood of Oscar Mayer bologna, Frito-Lay snack packs, and Jell-O pudding cups.

I'm glad to finally have Amanda talking. My nerves were so shot when she called (I'd left a message in the morning and since it was after seven, I figured she'd call me back the next day) that I could barely get my thoughts together. Luckily, though, after much nervous mumbling I've finally formed some decent questions.

One of my "good questions" concerns the pantry at her home. Amanda always shops seasonally, and advises that if you have a well-stocked pantry you can go to the market and find something in season, bring it home, and prepare it with something that acts as a "backdrop" to that ingredient. What might be a "backdrop" ingredient you'd keep in this well-stocked pantry? (That's my "good" question.)

"Well," says Amanda, "there's polenta, pasta, and rice. And it's good to have eggs, salt, olive oil, butter, dried red chiles, nutmeg, Parmesan, garlic, and other interesting spices, like smoked paprika."

"You could even use those by themselves to make dinner," I say eagerly. "Like pasta with butter, nutmeg, and Parmesan."

"Exactly," says Amanda. I am way impressive.

She also suggests that when it comes to spices, you should go all out. "You want to buy good spices," she says. "It makes a difference." She points out that those who follow the gospel of Alice Waters—a pioneer of the seasonal food movement—spare no expense when it comes to buying the best vegetables, fruits, and herbs, but frequently skimp when it comes to spices. "Especially when there is so much available online," she says, and she gives me the names of a number of sites: worldspice.com, le-sanctuaire.com, and kalustyan.com.

Eventually I ask her about growing up. Was her mom a cook? That's what leads to the revelations about the long food shopping experiences, her mom making everything from scratch. I tell her how opposite her childhood was from mine. "My mom always had a list and all we bought was processed food," I say. "My family kept Entenmann's, Fritos, and Chips Ahoy in business."

Amanda laughs and suddenly I realize something about myself: I am the victim of my upbringing. I may never master the market the way she can or the way others do, because for them the world of what's seasonal, what's fresh, what "looks good" has been created for them since birth. How can I train my eyes, my touch, and my sense of smell to embrace what's fresh and seasonal this late in the game?

What I need, I realize, is a coach. Someone who's a food gatherer by *nature,* who can show me the ropes. What I need, it becomes all too clear, is Stella Ragsdale.

Stella Ragsdale—a writer friend from writing school— grew up in the rural South: Tennessee, to be exact. Her family had an extensive garden with corn and squash and all other kinds of crops. They canned their own tomatoes.

So naturally, Stella shops at farmer's markets. She doesn't realize it, but she shops like a seasoned pro. She sniffs vegetables, and rejects those that are bruised or brown or moldy.

"I guess I do shop seasonally," she says when I call to enlist her. "I've been eating corn all month!"

Stella, it turns out, embodies the sort of shopper that every foodie should aspire to be. She shops seasonally, she shops without a list. And she does so without self-awareness, like Amanda Hesser's mother (and probably Amanda Hesser herself). Unlike me, or my mom, or most of my friends, or most of your friends, she doesn't ap-proach the supermarket with a specific course of action or plan. Her mind-set echoes that of Amanda's mother: "I'm going to see what looks good." She is a gatherer.

She's a gatherer, and she's also a frugal gatherer. For those of you reading this and thinking, "I'm on a budget:

I can't afford to just browse around farmer's markets shopping on a whim, I have a family to feed!" Stella should be your inspiration. She works two jobs to stay afloat. And yet she makes a point to eat well; and to eat well, she must shop well. Which is why I want her to be our teacher, this chapter's gatherer guru.

And so I ask Stella the gatherer to accompany me, Adam the hunter, on a trek through the farmer's market on a Friday morning.

"Okay," she agrees, "but I'm not sure that I really know anything."

We begin in the northwest section of the market, where the rows of market stands meet at the corner of their L-shape. It's 8 a.m.—another early morning—and stands are, once again, being set up.

"How do you want to start?" she asks.

"Let's just start walking and when something catches your eye, we'll stop and I'll observe you in action."

She gives me a perplexed look and then nods okay.

We start at a fruit stand and Stella spots cantaloupes.

"These look nice."

"What makes them look nice?"

She shrugs and then lifts one up. "They're firm." She sniffs: "And fragrant." Then she thumps it: "And they make a hollow sound when you thump them."

I quickly take notes: firm, fragrant, thump.

Then Stella spies corn.

"Normally, I'd pull back the husk to make sure there

aren't worms and that the kernels aren't dried up." I agree that it's unnecessary to do that now since we're not buying.

There's a large bin of beans and Stella starts thumbing through them. "We used to grow beans when I grew up. White runners and blue ribbons."

"Which are these?"

"White runners."

I nod as if to say "Of course! White runners!" and watch her examine the long vertical rods, much like Alain Ducasse examined the apricots on that first morning here a few weeks back. Her movements are impulsive and natural. She lifts a bean, quickly studies it, and quickly discards it. "This one's nice," she says, lifting a clean one.

"Why is it nice?" I press.

"There aren't any scars."

I look. I suppose it looks scarless, but I'm not sure I'd have thought to distinguish the scarred beans from the unscarred beans.

We continue. Tomatoes are prevalent and Stella lifts a few. "Tomatoes should be heavy—a little tender. I don't like unripe tomatoes."

I confess that I do like unripe tomatoes. "I don't like them mushy."

Stella shrugs that off and says that these tomatoes all look good. "Store tomatoes don't look like *anything*," she says by way of comparison.

"What does that mean?" I ask, a bit perplexed.

"They just don't look like anything."

This is the secret language of the gatherer. What she's articulating is something beyond me, beyond you, beyond anyone who didn't grow up in a world of tomatoes. And suddenly I begin to feel the same helplessness I felt when talking to Amanda Hesser. That revelation I made earlier—how my upbringing precludes me from mastering the market—begins to haunt me again. Who am I? What am I doing here?

Stella and I reach the end of the row of stalls and she asks me if I learned anything. "Yes," I say. "Thank you."

We go to breakfast and I have an omelet with American cheese. That's another thing we had in the fridge when I was growing up: American cheese. Could there be a cheese more representative of my upbringing, my limitations when it comes to food shopping? This overprocessed, neon-orange chemical muck: this is my brain when it comes to food shopping.

"Can I have a bite of that?" asks Stella.

"Sure, go ahead," I say.

American cheese isn't all bad, I suppose.

The truth is that there's no right or wrong when it comes to food shopping; there's no right or wrong when it comes to eating. So many forces are at play when we go to a store to buy food—economic, cultural, political, social, religious, geographic—that one can't, in good conscience, point to a conventional food shopper and say, "Change your ways or I won't marry you!" Marriage is a serious institution, and refusing marriage to someone based on how he goes food shopping is like refusing marriage for what someone wears or how he combs his hair or what shows he watches on TV. These behaviors are deeply rooted in who we are as people, how we are raised, and our current living conditions.

But in this age of fast food, frozen food, and Fresh Direct (Internet food delivery), we've lost a connection with our food and where it comes from. One nice thing you can say about the farmer's market is that when you're at a stand scrutinizing summer squash, as Stella was, you're in a position to interact directly with the person who grew that squash. You can ask him questions. He can give you tips. And there's something wonderfully personal about it, like having a friend bake you a cake from scratch on your birthday. There may be eggshell in it, but it's made with love.

So on a peaceful Wednesday afternoon, I am coming back from a drab breakfast of bagel and cream cheese and processed orange juice. I am walking through the market and I spy a tomato stand. There are red tomatoes and yellow tomatoes of different sizes and shades. I think: "I could make some kind of salad for lunch." I buy two red tomatoes and two yellow ones. I also buy a big bunch of basil.

When I get home, I wash the tomatoes and slice them thickly with a serrated knife. One of the tomatoes is quite unripe—the insides are still a bit green. But the others are lovely. I lay them on a plate, and wash and dry the basil leaves. I put a basil leaf between every two tomatoes and then drizzle the whole thing with olive oil and a few drops of balsamic vinegar. A little salt and pepper and lunch is ready. The verdict? Delicious, of course.

That night, for dinner, I take the leftover basil and make a pesto. It couldn't be easier. In my food processor, I place a quarter cup of pine nuts, a handful of walnuts, and a few cloves of garlic. I pulse that together and then add a big bunch of basil leaves, some salt, and pepper. While the processor's running, I drizzle in about ½ cup of olive oil and then add about ⅓ cup of freshly grated Parmesan, pulse again, and I'm done.

If you're trying this, next you boil some spaghetti or spaghettini. (Add these to your list of things Amanda Hesser suggested that you have in your pantry, along with walnuts and pine nuts.) When it's done, drain it and spoon on the pesto. A terrific dinner, indeed.

And right away, there are two meals from one casual trip to the farmer's market.

After this success, I make several trips back. On my next trip I am a bit more adventurous. I stop at a goat's-milk stand and buy goat's-milk yogurt. At a honey stand, I talk with the honey purveyors about my choices.

"Each honey name is based on what flower the bees pollinate," a kind woman explains.

"Which is your favorite?" I ask.

"Here," she says, grabbing a toothpick. "Try the goldenrod."

She opens a jar of goldenrod honey and dips the toothpick in. She hands it to me. It is surprisingly floral and sweet, yet subtle. I buy the bottle.

I also buy some raspberries from the Asian man's berry stand (I don't taste them like that woman did, but I do wear army boots), and when I get home I make a snack of goat's-milk yogurt, goldenrod honey, and fresh raspberries. It is most unusual and highly enjoyable.

Since then, there've been salads with fresh arugula and just-ripe nectarines; creamy, compact slices of Coach Farm goat cheese; giant loaves of sourdough purchased from one of the market's many bakers. Might I be a gatherer after all?

My favorite coffee shop in New York, where we begin our next chapter, has a store only two blocks away from the farmer's market. In the olden days, after finishing my coffee, I'd circumvent the market and make my way home by way of Sixth Avenue. But these days, I make a point to walk through the market, despite my heavy bookbag or the drizzly weather. When I go, I don't really have an agenda—perhaps I can use some fruit and veggies for the week. Maybe I'll make a salad for dinner. Some cheese would be nice to have. I could buy some flowers for the kitchen table. But maybe I'll surprise myself and buy farm-raised chicken or fresh organic eggs. My attitude is a good one and simply articulated.

I'm going to see what looks good.

THREE

Expand Your Palate

Lisa lifts the iced vanilla latte to her lips and, for a moment, I believe with great conviction that after she takes a sip she'll throw her head back in ecstasy, moan erotically, and yell with frightening force: "Oh, Adam, my darling, my dear friend, you've done it! You've changed me—I'm a new woman—I love coffee!"

The chances of this happening, however, are so minute, so far-fetched, that Don Quixote himself, if he knew Lisa, would scoff at my ridiculous ambition. For Lisa is like a windmill in the distance, a giant force in my food consciousness, a force that spins its arms in circular motions, batting away three detested food items: olives, smelly cheese, and coffee.

As long as I've known her, Lisa has passionately advocated her disgust for these items. "Olives are just wrong," she will say. "People who like olives are sick." Smelly cheese also eludes her. "Ugh," she grumbles. "Why would anyone eat that?"

Mostly, though, it's coffee that baffles her. She is convinced that the world's reliance on and enjoyment of coffee—the entire coffee culture itself—are the product of an undiagnosed mental illness or some mass hypnotism. "I just don't get why so many people drink coffee," she says as we sit down at Joe: The Art of Coffee, my favorite coffee shop in New York. "What's wrong with them?"

I have developed a strategy here. Lisa detests coffee so much that I figure why not confront her with the most intense, most unpleasant coffee experience first, and then reward her with the most oversugared, candylike coffee drink in return? I will force upon her a shot of espresso—a pure, concentrated, reddened, tiny cup of coffee essence—and then, when she's gagging and cursing my existence, I will present to her a nice tall glass of milk with an espresso shot and vanilla syrup (aka an iced vanilla latte). The plan should work brilliantly.

I consult my friends at the counter, Josh and Brenden.

"I don't know, man," says Josh. "Espresso is nasty if you don't like coffee."

"Why don't you give her a macchiato?" asks Brenden. "It's a little less intense."

"Yeah," says Josh. "Macchiatos are a little sweeter."

Clearly Josh and Brenden don't understand my plan. I want Lisa to suffer with her first drink so that the second drink will be a sweet reward. If she mildly enjoys the first drink, the second drink won't offer such a dramatic contrast. How else can I expand her palate? So I order an espresso shot and moments later it is ready. I carry it over to the table where Lisa is sitting.

The man sitting next to us can't help but observe what is happening.

"She doesn't like coffee and you're giving her an espresso shot?" he comments. "That's just cruel, man."

Lisa stares down at the shiny red liquid.

"I already know I'm going to hate it," she says. "It smells awful."

"Go ahead," I say. "It's not going to kill you."

If there were a video camera available to document the next moment, students of art, psychology, and theater would battle over the tape to study the brilliant display of emotions that flow vibrantly across Lisa's face. As she takes a sip, shades of pain and disgust morph into hollow expressions of existential doubt and, at the end, a keen awareness of death. "Oh," she moans. "It's horrible. It's so horrible."

"What does it taste like?" I ask intently, pad and paper in hand.

"Mud," she says, stifling tears. "But like offensive mud. Strong mud." She stares desperately at a water tank with free plastic cups. "Can I get water?" she begs.

"No," I say. "I'm going to get you an iced vanilla latte."

I return to the counter.

"What did she think?" asks Josh.

"She hated it," I say.

He and Brenden laugh. "We told you," says Brenden.

"An iced vanilla latte," I order. "Stat!"

"Here," I say to Lisa, moments later, presenting her with the tall glass of soothing vanilla coffee milk.

She looks at it, looks at me, and—exasperated—takes a sip.

And it is in this moment—the moment between her sipping and her reacting—that this chapter's agenda lives. For we are at the next step in our journey: the broadening of the palate, the freeing of the mouth. To expand one's palate is to expand one's mind, to open oneself up to new experience, to new sensation. Those of us who are stubborn about what we eat, who refuse to try new things, are in a perpetual state of bratty adolescence. "I hate Brussels sprouts," your inner brat says when you see Brussels sprouts on a menu. "They're nasty."

What your inner brat doesn't know is that Brussels sprouts, when coated in olive oil, roasted deep brown, and sprinkled with salt, can be better than french fries. So your inner brat will shape the person you become as you grow older, a person who hates Brussels sprouts. Or, in the case of Lisa, a person who hates coffee, olives, and stinky cheese.

Lisa is a person who, one might say, is stuck in her ways.

For example, Lisa is a vegetarian. She has been a vegetarian since she was eleven. Her vegetarianism is as much a part of who she is as her ability to play Tetris like a master, to clear a Minesweeper board in seconds, or to make sock puppets with her mom. The Lisa of today is the same Lisa I knew in college: she's feisty, funny, manic, and peppy.

She's also super talented—a terrific singer, actress, and comedian—and what frustrates me to no end is that Lisa has worked an unfulfilling job for the past six years. Like many people our age, she feels a bit trapped. She wants to go out there and do the things she loves to do—the things she's dreamed about—but she needs to pay the bills. So she does what she must do: day in, day out. I want her to go out there and conquer the world but she's reined in by a sense of duty and habit.

Which is why my desire to broaden her palate is a heartfelt one. I strongly believe that the relationship between what we eat and who we are is a deep one; if Lisa can break her eating habits, maybe she can break her life habits too. I'm convinced that by learning to like olives or coffee or cheese she can render herself less passive, more daring, more empowered.

Lisa and I enter Snack Taverna, the first stop—before coffee, before cheese—on our tour of Food Lisa Hates. A beautiful, sunny Greek restaurant on Bedford Street in the West Village, Snack Taverna is perfect for the olive portion of our quest, because the Greeks worship the olive and olives are featured prominently on the menu.

"Okay," I say, "we're going to get the Greek salad with kalamata olives."

"Can we get the olives on the side?" asks Lisa. "Otherwise they'll contaminate everything they touch."

"No," I reply. "And we'll share the roasted vegetable sandwich with olive tapenade."

"But I don't like tapenade," grumbles Lisa.

"Precisely," I say. "That's why I'm making you eat it."

Minutes after we order, the waiter arrives with a giant bowl of the freshest-looking Greek salad you've ever seen and a sandwich slathered with olivey goodness. "Bon appétit," he says.

Glistening on top of the freshly cut tomatoes, onions, and cucumbers are two or three kalamata olives. I look Lisa in the eye and then I look at the olive and then back at Lisa. "Okay," I say. "Try an olive."

Kalamata are my favorite olives. Fruity, firm, and juicy, kalamata olives are the perfect transitional tool for converting an olive-hater into an olive-lover. They're not as mealy as those black salad bar olives, not as intense as the dark green olives they plop into cocktails. Lisa is certain to acknowledge at least some semblance of enjoyment as she nibbles.

"I can see why people might think this is good," she says after a moment. "But it's just not for me. Olives and I are not meant to be."

"Fine," I say. "Try the tapenade."

She takes a bite of the sandwich. The sandwich is on lovely toasted French bread and has roasted eggplant, squash, and peppers. She chews, swallows, and then announces: "It tastes like olives. Not that I *hate* the way it tastes," she continues. "I mean, I can tolerate it. I just don't like it."

Tolerate is not a word one wants to hear in the context

of food. Would you tell a hardworking cook that you "tolerated" her food after she served you a five-course meal? Of course you wouldn't. That would break her heart. And as Lisa scrapes the tapenade off the top half of her sandwich and picks around the olives in the salad, I feel my heart break a little. I've failed in the first part of my mission: Lisa has rejected the olive and her palate hasn't expanded an inch.

Lisa isn't alone, though, when it comes to her static tastes: my tastes were destined to be just as static. I come from a father who hates cheese. *Hates*. Nothing makes my dad more miserable than the smell or taste of cheese. He orders Caesar salad without the cheese; he immediately dismisses any busboy or waiter who approaches him with a hunk of cheese and grater in hand. For years he refused to return to Balthazar, the trendy Manhattan bistro, because the French onion soup had such a strong smell of cheese. And no one at our table even ordered French onion soup—he sniffed it several tables over.

Expanding my father's palate would be an impossible mission. His hatred of cheese is a pillar of his personality, an essential part of who he is. And as Lisa and I enter Artisanal, a cheese restaurant on Thirty-second Street, I'm suddenly forced to confront the truth about myself: I am, at heart, my father's son. This restaurant terrifies me.

"I don't really hate cheese," says Lisa. "I mean, there are certain cheeses I like and certain cheeses I don't like."

"Well, we're here to get you over it," I say, masking my own fear.

As we're led to a table, I begin to recall childhood sleep-overs where someone's mother would be cooking lasagna and I'd have to feign illness to explain why I was mushing it all around my plate. Or how watching a waiter make fet-tuccine Alfredo would give me nightmares for weeks: all that cream and white gooey cheese. We once saw a waiter prepare it in a giant Parmesan wheel. I was traumatized.

How did I get over my terror of cheese? Am I really over it? What were the initial steps?

Maybe it started with Parmesan. I bought fresh Parmesan for a recipe and I slowly acclimated myself to it. Once I got the idea of it—acknowledging, like Lisa did with olives, how other people might find it enjoyable—I was able to in-corporate cheese more and more into my diet. Like a diver slowly rising to the surface so he doesn't get the bends, I worked my way up gradually. My latest feat had been an accord with blue cheese. I could accept blue cheese in sal-ads with beets as long as it wasn't the overdry, brittle blue you find on salad bars.

Yet, only a few months back, I had another traumatic cheese experience. I was with my mother at the notable TriBeCa restaurant Chanterelle. We ordered a tasting menu and when it came to the cheese course, the waitress brought over a tremendous cart arrayed—like a museum piece—with giant blocks of cheese. She described all of our choices and Mom and I, utterly baffled, asked her if she would choose our cheese for us.

"My pleasure," said the waitress.

She took slivers of tall creamy cheeses, darker golden cheeses, and rich, pungent blue cheeses and laid them on two separate plates. Just when we thought she was done she reached under the cart and removed a canister.

"This," she said, "is *very* special."

She unscrewed the lid and revealed a bubbling, gurgling mass. The waitress spooned this substance onto our plates and said, "Enjoy."

The stink was unbearable. And the taste—for I did taste it—was like death on a spoon. How could *anyone*, anyone in her right mind, enjoy this? This was the essence of badness, the very thing we seek to avoid when we eat. I couldn't then and can't now understand the appeal of putting such unpleasantness in one's mouth. It seems to be the antithesis of all that is wonderful about eating.

These feelings make ordering at Artisanal all the more challenging. I want to push Lisa to her limits but I want to protect myself from revealing my hypocrisy.

"Well, we have to get the fondue," I say. "Everyone says to get the fondue."

The fondue at Artisanal features four cheese options: the classic Swiss, the Artisanal blend, fondues du jour, and the very intense, very hard-core Stilton (a wildly pungent blue) and Sauterne (a sweet dessert wine).

"Stilton and Sauterne," I tell the waitress, who warns that it's the most intense. "You have to really like cheese to enjoy it," she explains.

"Sold," I say bravely.

We begin with Parmesan gnocchi, which is terrific, and then gougeres—little cheese puffs that we pop into our mouths quite happily. We have a salad of beets and goat cheese. And then it arrives: a giant stinky vat of gurgling, bubbling blue cheese with a burner underneath to keep the whole thing going.

"Wow, that's hot," I say, leaning over the vat.

The waitress brings us bread cubes and little vegetables to dip. "Enjoy," she says.

Lisa dips a bread cube in. I follow. We taste. We eye each other.

"Well," she says, "it's not horrible."

I continue to chew. Who am I? Am I a static character? Should I relent and admit that this isn't my favorite, or is change possible—can I grow while chewing this weird, pungent mix of cheese and bread? Yes, it's unpleasant to me, it tastes like rot and decay, it reminds me a bit of death. But perhaps that's part of its charm. Perhaps tasting death is a good thing, a reminder that we're mortal, that we're all vats of cream, sumptuous and sweet, that fester as we grow older until we are wrinkled and flecked with blue veins. This vat of blue cheese offers wisdom and I must humble myself before it to receive its message. And, when I think of it that way, I do like it: I like it for its depth, its complexity, the way it challenges me.

"I like it," I say. "It's really interesting."

"Yes," says Lisa, as she blows on another cube. "At least it's not as bad as coffee."

• • •

Lisa hates the iced vanilla latte.

"It tastes like coffee," she says matter-of-factly, as if this were the obvious inevitable conclusion to her coffee challenge.

"But don't you taste the vanilla syrup? The milk?"

"No," she says. "I just taste coffee."

"Here," I say as I pour sugar syrup from a bottle into the glass. I stir it around. "Now try."

She sips and says, "Now it just tastes like very, very sweet coffee."

I am spent. I led the horse to coffee, I made her drink, and nothing changed. What more could I do?

"Let's try it on different areas of your tongue," I suggest. "Different parts of your tongue receive things differently."

She puts her finger on top of the straw and lifts the liquid onto the front of her tongue. She lets go. She swallows.

"Nope," she says. "Still tastes like coffee."

She tries it on the center, on the back, the back right, the back left. No good. Still tastes like coffee.

"And it's not like I don't want to like coffee," Lisa offers. "I'm jealous of people who go out for coffee. It's a big part of being social."

"Well, at least you gave it a fair shot," I say, resigned.

"Yeah," says Lisa, "and if people go out for coffee I can always order a hot chocolate."

I think about this for a second. If Lisa can have a hot

chocolate, why should she drink coffee? What's she really missing out on—is coffee really that special?

The answer is that it's not. Lisa's character is defined by the foods she likes and doesn't like, just as much as it's defined by the people she surrounds herself with, the books she chooses to read, and the TV shows she chooses to watch. My dad is the same way: his distaste for cheese is an ineluctable part of who he is. Lisa and my dad are static characters when it comes to food: chances are they'll feel the same way about food tomorrow as they do today. That's their right.

What matters, ultimately, is the effort. Growing pains are a natural fact of life: it hurts to grow. It hurts for someone who hates coffee to drink a shot of espresso; for a person who hates olives to eat a kalamata. We should applaud Lisa for her efforts here today and congratulate her on a job well done.

And the story might have ended here, but a few weeks later Lisa and I are at another restaurant, one not even known for olives. And she is eating a goat cheese salad with toast topped with goat cheese and kalamata olives. Without preparing me first, Lisa leaves the olives on her toast and takes a bite.

"Whoah!" I yelp. "Did you just do what I think you did?"

"I did," she says as she chews.

"And?"

She pauses for a moment.

"Actually," she says, "I like it. It tastes good in combination with everything else."

Call me crazy, but I hear chains crack on Lisa's tongue and see a blast of light shoot forth from her lips. I keep quiet and nod my approval; I don't want to spoil the moment.

When the plates are cleared, the waitress asks us if we want coffee. I look at Lisa hopefully.

"No, thank you," she says. "Just a check."

Change takes time: we don't become new people overnight. Yet Lisa, who remains the same delightful person I knew in college, but who works a job that doesn't let her shine the way she deserves to shine, now knows that change is possible. All it takes is an olive and a dream.

FOUR

Cross Cultures

As a young man I was enchanted not with the work of Tolstoy or Dickens but was instead taken by the prominent prose stylings of Blanche Knotts, author of *Truly Tasteless Jokes,* volumes I, II, III, IV, and most significantly: V. I would beg my mother to buy me the various volumes I saw each time we went to the bookstore and she, without too much concern, bought them for me. Comedy was a huge discovery for me: I learned, very early on, that if I memorized these jokes and told them to the kids at school they would like me.

So I would stay up at night and recite them to myself until I had them memorized. It didn't matter if I understood them. I remember one in particular that to this day I don't quite get. It involved a woman whose vagina is somehow sealed who must be rocked back and forth. That was the punch line: rock her back and forth. It made little sense then and it makes little sense now. Rock her back and forth? What does it *mean*?

But I didn't care. I'd tell the jokes on class trips and my friends—for they were now my friends because I was funny—would squeal with laughter.

"What's long and green and smells like Miss Piggy?" I'd ask.

"What?" they'd beg.

"Kermit's finger!"

We'd howl and we had no idea what we were talking about. Or maybe they did—I had no idea.

An unfortunate side effect, though, was that in addition to the sex jokes these books contained *ethnic* jokes. So after a rousing round of "rock her back and forth" and "Kermit's finger," I'd pepper my humor with Polish jokes, black jokes, and Asian jokes.

"What's a Chinese blindfold?" I'd ask.

"What?"

"Dental floss!"

Howls and screams. I was a champion. There was no stopping me.

That is until, a few years later, I was reciting my best memorized jokes to a new group of high school friends on a class trip.

"That's hilarious," said a rotund Irish guy named Pat.

"Thank you," I said.

"What's the difference between a Jew and a pizza?" he said.

"What?" I asked.

"A pizza doesn't scream when you put it in an oven."

It took me a moment to get what the joke was referencing: Jews? Ovens? And then, suddenly, and for the first time ever in the brief history of my life, I was completely silenced.

My freshman hall at Emory University was 90 percent Indian. I'd call home every day and report my adventures with my new Indian friends, whose names I had to repeat three or four times before my parents learned them. Shivani, Sunil, Vearthen, Priya, Payal, Vikas—these were my first ambassadors to the world beyond Blanche Knotts, the world of the "other" that my sheltered upbringing kept me apart from.

I remember my first Indian meal with them. I had no idea what any of this stuff was. Naan? What's naan? And why does everything taste like curry?

Soon, though, I realized something interesting: I was as exotic to them as they were to me.

"Why do you celebrate Passover?" they'd ask.

"Because . . . during the plagues the Jews spread lamb's blood on their doors to spare their firstborn from the angel of death."

"Oh," they'd say, still slightly baffled.

I never really knew, growing up in Long Island and Boca Raton, Florida, how odd Jewish people were to many people in other parts of the country and beyond. I got a taste of it in Irish Pat's joke, but I didn't truly experience my otherness until I left home.

My Jewish heritage, I discovered, is a big part of me. I may not go to synagogue on Friday night but I can't shake off my Jewishness any more than I can shake off my wholehearted love for *Pippin* on DVD. These are the things that make me who I am.

So for this chapter I have devised a scheme: I will choose a friend whose culture is still foreign to me, still exotic, and who knows as little about Judaism as I know about her culture. Once this person is selected, I will have her share the foods and rituals of her culture, and I will share the foods and rituals of mine. But whom will I choose? Who is still an "other" to me?

Enter Patty Jang.

Patty is my friend from writing school. She is a lesbian, a bicyclist, a playwright, and a food enthusiast. She also happens to be Korean, which makes her a perfect selection for my project.

And so on a Sunday afternoon after the World Cup, Patty leads me up Broadway and across Thirty-second Street. We are only blocks away from my Chelsea apartment and suddenly we're in another world. "This is K-Town," declares Patty amid a large cluster of Korean restaurants and grocery stores.

"Wow," I say. "I had no idea this was so close to where I live."

We stroll past Korean families pushing Korean children in Korean strollers.

"This is where I take my mom when she comes to New York," says Patty. "She likes it better than the K-Town in Philadelphia."

Soon we reach our first destination on Patty's tour of Korean culture: Ha Ah Reum, a grocery store where she plans to buy ingredients for the dinner she's cooking the next night.

"What will you be making?" I ask.

"Kimchi Bi-Bim Pahp," she says.

"Ummm," I murmur. "Can you spell that?"

I know nothing about Korean food. I've never eaten it. Even if I tried to eat it, I wouldn't know what to order. And even if I knew what to order, I wouldn't know if what was placed in front of me was good, bad, or even edible. This is the culinary equivalent of learning a new language or, more accurately, a new breathing pattern. If eating is a natural process, then eating what is unfamiliar feels *unnatural*. This is why so many of us rarely venture outside our comfort zones.

Patty grabs a basket and we make our way up the aisles of Ha Ah Reum.

The entrance has stacks of what must be a very popular brand of rice—"Kokoho" rice. Then, in a refrigerated section, I observe lots of canned coffee drinks.

"Koreans love canned coffee drinks," explains Patty. "Especially Nescafé."

She grabs a sweet yogurt drink that she liked growing up. And she begins loading up on items whose existence I never even fathomed: royal fern stems, pickled radish, bean sprouts. (Okay, I've fathomed bean sprouts.)

"Wow. I've never even heard of half this stuff."

"Well, this is what we cook with."

"Cool. I'm going to go explore."

I make my way to the snack food aisle and delight over bags of sweet-potato candy, shrimp-flavored potato chips, and dried anchovies with almonds. I remove that last bag from the shelf and resolve to buy it.

"I'll take these home," I say to myself. "And learn to snack like a Korean."

Additionally, I take a bag of bean cakes and dried squid. Patty, who's caught up, says that dried squid is really popular to snack on. "I used to eat it all the time."

Then we pass a shelf of Spam and Patty informs me, "Koreans love Spam." I do not buy any Spam.

We make our way out the door and I gladden over my Korean snack food bounty.

A week later, at the beginning of the Jewish portion of our exercise, Patty and Stella (the gatherer from chapter 2, who's tagged along) are staring at me as I gobble chopped liver at Katz's Deli. The look on their faces is clear: *these foods are bizarre.*

"This dinner is fechactamamie," says Stella with her Southern drawl, employing the Yiddish word I taught her earlier in the evening.

"It is not," I reply.

"Can I put ketchup on these?" asks Stella, indicating the potato pancakes.

"No!" I implore. "Use the applesauce and sour cream."

"But I want ketchup," she whimpers.

Patty is more generous. She kindly samples the chopped liver and furrows her brow as she chews: "It tastes more like onions than liver," she observes. Then a moment later, "Now I taste the liver. It takes a moment and then it hits you."

Chopped liver is a staple from my childhood. My grandmother used to warn: "It's an organ meat," whenever we'd order it. I'm not quite sure what her warning meant but the implication was that chopped liver was unhealthy. Therefore, my brother and I wanted more of it.

"I can't believe you like eating liver," says Stella, poking around the potato pancakes. Stella is a vegetarian.

"You dip the corned beef in the mustard?" asks Patty. I am teaching her how to eat a Katz's corned beef sandwich. Because it is packed so thickly, I advise eating the top half with a fork and the rest like a sandwich. I squirt mustard onto the side of the plate so that each forkful can be dipped in mustard before being consumed.

"Yes," I say. "The mustard is what makes it great."

Sharing this bit of my culture is reciprocation for the earlier part of the week when Patty shared with me bits and pieces of her Korean culture.

"I like it," says Patty, swallowing some corned beef.

Stella is silent. She is not an official participant of the "Cross Cultures" chapter.

Fade back to K-Town, where Patty and I stand outside of Kunjip, a Korean barbecue restaurant, watching throngs of Koreans and their families waiting to get in or leaving—it's difficult to tell. We put our name on the list and we're told the wait is ten to fifteen minutes.

"Maybe after dinner we can have Pot Bin Su," says Patty, as we wait outside.

"What is it?" I query.

"It's shaved ice with sweetened red beans and fruit. I love it."

As I look around me—at the Korean families, the grocery store, a Korean coffee shop—I feel like I've penetrated a secret world. True, there are white people too—Korean barbecue is far less exotic to people who've grown up in less sheltered environments. But even so, the large majority of people are Korean and I feel as though during the six-block walk up from my apartment I have journeyed across an ocean. This is the miracle of leaping out of your comfort zone—you are transported beyond your realm to somewhere new.

"They're ready," says Patty, who sees the hostess waving us over.

We go into the door and wait on another line, a smaller

one. The hostess says something to Patty in Korean and Patty says, "They want us to order now."

We quickly flip open the menu and Patty points to a dish at the top—Gal Bi Gui, grilled boneless short ribs marinated in soy sauce—and orders it for two. She also orders two OB beers.

Soon we are led to a table and Patty explains how it works. "A Korean meal starts with panchan," she explains.

"Panchan?"

"Yes, panchan," she continues. "A lot of little dishes—like tapas, or appetizers. You might get kimchi, anchovies, squid, egg, potatoes."

As if on cue, a waiter appears with our beer and a clay pot. He sets down the beers and then the clay pot. In the pot is egg—baked, like a soufflé—and sizzling in sesame oil, seasoned with just salt and pepper. Then comes more panchan: sautéed bean sprouts, seaweed, cabbage kimchi, radish kimchi, fish cakes, and microgreens.

"Try the kimchi. This is a Korean staple."

I've heard of kimchi, I've read about it, and I know of its existence, but I've never tasted it. Now I lift a piece of the radish kimchi to my lips—studying its vibrant red color—and I taste.

"Well?" asks Patty.

"I like it," I say and I'm not lying, though I'm not quite telling the truth. It tastes wildly unfamiliar yet strangely inevitable, as if this were one of the major food groups I missed out on when I first discovered food. There's heat, there's crunch, there's tang. "It's really interesting," I conclude.

"Ah," says Patty. "Here comes the beef."

A platter of raw beef is placed before us and then a waiter arrives with a hot plate for us to cook it on. But because our table is small, they take the hot plate to a separate table and cook the beef for us there. When they return, they set down the beef and Patty teaches me how to assemble the various raw materials before us.

"You take the lettuce, add some rice, then some spicy sauce, then the meat, and some scallions."

I assemble the package, wrapping it all up in a lettuce leaf, and take a bite. The flavors immediately pop in my mouth as I groan—or rather, "mmmm"—with pleasure.

"Isn't it good?" asks Patty.

For Patty this is more meaningful than just a cultural show-and-tell for some Jewish friend's book. Patty, who is twenty-nine, hasn't had beef since she was seventeen. She recently started eating meat again because her vegetarian girlfriend, Lauren, was diagnosed as anemic and the doctor suggested she eat meat to regain her health. Patty agreed to join Lauren as they crossed back over to Meat Land. This allowed her to return to the culture she grew up with.

"Korean barbecue was the only food I liked growing up," she says after we order Pot Bin Su, her favorite Korean dessert, later in the evening at a Korean café. "Otherwise my mom would cook my brother and me American food and then cook Korean food for herself and my dad."

Two years ago, Patty's father died of lung cancer. This was the first time she'd eaten beef since his death, and doing so floods her with memories.

"I remember him at restaurants," she says. "He would order hot-pot casserole soup—Katchisan—anchovy paste soup, and it was very spicy. He would sit there over his bowl and sweat."

Patty laughs and together we share a memory that this food has afforded us. Then a waiter comes out with a giant bowl holding what looks like a mammoth banana split. At the center is shaved ice and on top are fruit and sweet beans surrounding a big scoop of vanilla ice cream.

"Try to get it all on your spoon at once," instructs Patty.

So I dig in—scooping on some ice, some beans, some fruit, and some ice cream. Naturally it is wonderful and I smile.

Patty smiles back: it's her favorite dessert.

Whether you're Jewish or Korean, it's intimidating to enter a restaurant where you can't read the menu, to travel to a new country where you can't speak the language, to order a dish that you can't decipher. Many people (my parents included) choose to travel the world on cruise ships because they can quite contentedly return to the ship for dinner. (My parents have friends who pride themselves for "only eating on the ship.") Crossing cultures is an internal journey as much as an external one: you can physically stand in Paris but choose to eat at a McDonald's. It's the tearing down of internal walls that allows for the true journey to begin. Fear is what holds us back, and fear is preventing Stella from getting a soda at Katz's.

"Stella. Take your ticket and go to the soda counter and ask for a soda."

"No," says Stella.

"Why not?"

"I'm scared."

Katz's is an old-fashioned deli with old-fashioned rules. To get your food, you bring your ticket to the counter, you ask for what you want, and they punch it—you pay on the way out. There are separate counters for desserts, sandwiches, hot dogs, and soda. We are at the sandwich counter, and Stella refuses to move alone to the soda counter.

"Stella, just go to the counter," I beg.

"No," she says petulantly.

"Why not?"

Stella doesn't say anything but I see that she is intimidated. For her, a rural Tennessean, nothing could be more exotic than New York Jews selling soda behind a counter.

"Here, Stella," says Patty. "I'll go with you."

Patty, we should note again, is an official participant of the "Cross Cultures" chapter.

• • •

Patty and Lauren's apartment is a five-flight walk-up in Park Slope, Brooklyn, and it's a blisteringly hot summer day. Inside, it's even hotter than outside—the stove is on and Patty isn't running the A/C.

"Please, Patty," I beg. "Please, turn the A/C on."

"Quit your bitching," she chastises.

"I'm Jewish," I explain. "This is what we do—we kvetch."

Patty, after a few more kvetches, finally concedes, puts the A/C on, and returns to her task. She is sautéeing mushrooms for the main dish she is preparing—Kimchi Bi-Bim Pahp. Meanwhile she puts me to work rolling and cutting the kim-pahp, a sushilike dish very popular in Korea.

"How is this different from sushi?" I ask.

"I'm not sure," says Patty. "Maybe what's inside it?"

Inside it are carrots, crab sticks, and pickled radish. There's no wasabi and no soy sauce.

The cookbook Patty is using, *Vignettes of Korean Cooking,* is by a Korean woman Patty met on a trip to Korea she took with her mother earlier this year. "She's very, very rich," gossips Patty. "But she's also very generous. There were seventy-five of us on the trip" (the trip was for alumni of Patty's mother's college) "and she took us all out to this seafood restaurant and bought kim-pahp for all of us. There were huge platters. It was the freshest I've ever had."

At this point, I've finished my task and I'm looking at pictures from Patty's trip. The women (the trip is mostly women) are all smiling and dressed like my grandmother and her friends might dress: floral patterns, sunglasses, large hats.

"It's funny how all moms and grandmothers look alike across cultures."

"It's true," agrees Patty, who has now cracked an egg and added it to the pot.

"Was this your first time in Korea?"

"No," she says. "I'd gone two times before. Once when I was thirteen and again when I was twenty-one."

"What was it like?"

"Well," she says, "the first time I was eaten alive by mosquitoes. There was no shower—just a drain in the middle of the bathroom."

"Yikes," I say. Jewish people much prefer real showers to drains in the bathroom.

Then Patty tells a story about the morning she ate cereal for breakfast—"there was no regular milk, just goat's milk"—and she thought the goat's milk in her cereal was "disgusting." Right after that the family loaded into a car to drive to a Korean folk village for a family portrait. They sat in Seoul traffic for hours—"the traffic there is terrible"—and she got more and more carsick. When they finally got out of the car and got into family portrait formation (it was a huge portrait, with all sorts of relatives), Patty sprung forward and puked all over the ground.

"It was awful," says Patty, laughing. "My poor aunt cleaned it all up with a napkin."

Just then Lauren comes home and Patty announces the completion of dinner.

"Come and get it," she says and places the Kimchi Bi-Bim Pahp on a table on the floor. Here's the recipe:

Kimchi Bi-Bim Pahp
Rice Topped with Kimchi and Vegetables

From *Vignettes of Korean Cooking,*
by S. Jae-Ok Chang

Makes 6 servings

2 tablespoons sesame oil for kimchi and
   mushrooms
2 cups kimchi (available in Korean specialty
   groceries), well fermented, rinsed of seasoning,
   squeezed, and cut in strips
1/4 cup seasoned kimchi, well fermented, cut in
   strips
8 dried shiitake mushrooms, softened in warm
   water and cut in strips
1 egg, slightly beaten
1 cup cooked bean sprouts
1 tablespoon toasted sesame seeds
Pinch garlic salt
2 tablespoons sesame oil for fern stems

2 cups royal fern stems, rinsed, drained, gently
    squeezed, and cut into 1-inch lengths
$1/2$ tablespoon soy sauce
1 tablespoon toasted sesame seeds
$1/4$ teaspoon Hon-da-shi powder
1 whole green onion, chopped
1 cup lean ground beef
1 tablespoon soy sauce
$1/4$ teaspoon black pepper
1 teaspoon sugar
6 cups cooked white or brown rice
3 toasted seaweed sheets, crumbled with fingers
Hot Korean chile paste, optional

SEASONING:
3 tablespoons soy sauce
3 tablespoons sesame oil
3 tablespoons toasted sesame seeds

In a skillet, heat 2 tablespoons sesame oil, then stir-fry both kinds of kimchi and black mushrooms 2 minutes. Push to the sides, fry the egg in the center, combine, and remove to a dish. Mix bean sprouts, 1 tablespoon toasted sesame seeds, and garlic salt. Heat 2 tablespoons sesame oil in a skillet, stir-fry fern stems, season with $1/2$ tablespoon soy sauce, 1 tablespoon toasted sesame seeds, $1/4$ teaspoon Hon-da-shi powder, and chopped green onion. Remove. Stir-fry beef until browned, then season with 1 tablespoon soy sauce, ¼ teaspoon black pepper, and 1 teaspoon sugar. Mix seasoning ingredients. In an individual serving bowl, place 1 cup rice, top with kimchi mixture, and arrange bean sprouts, fern stems, and beef to cover rice. Sprinkle crumbled seaweed on top. At the table, add seasoning to taste, including hot Korean chile paste as desired.

The assemblage of textures, flavors, and colors on the plates before us is really beautiful. I draw a little diagram in the notebook on my lap: a giant circle and on the top the royal ferns, clockwise to the right kimchi (cabbage and radish), then the shiitakes, squid, sautéed beef, egg, bean sprouts, and seaweed. I attempt to use chopsticks but fail when it comes to the rice.

"Patty?" I say with embarrassment.

"Yes?" she replies.

"Can I have . . ."

"A spoon?"

"Yes."

Lauren rolls her eyes as Patty rises to get me a spoon.

"Jewish people," I explain, "have *functional* utensils."

"I'm half Jewish," returns Lauren. "And I use chopsticks fine."

She demonstrates her Jewish chopstick prowess and I

applaud her. Then I take the spoon from Patty and finish my dinner. I enjoy it thoroughly.

A few weeks later, on a trip to Washington, D.C., I am at the Holocaust Museum. In a room with an elaborate diorama of a gas chamber, videos of Nazi doctor experiments, and a wooden train car sitting on real railroad tracks from Auschwitz, perhaps it is surprising that the exhibit I find the most moving, the one that really hits me the hardest, is a simple glass display with cooking equipment. On the second floor, which focuses on concentration camps, I find myself face-to-face with spatulas, spoons, bowls, and graters.

The graters are the most troubling. What did these Jews—Polish Jews who were told to pack a suitcase in anticipation of relocation, never knowing they were heading to their death—plan to do with graters? Would they grate potatoes for potato pancakes? Would they grate horseradish to eat with their beef or herring? Why *graters*?

The link between those poor souls and myself lives in the secret of those graters. Their tastes are echoed in mine: they, like me, probably salivated for smoked fish, bellowed for bagels, and swooned over sweet noodle pudding. The taste of these foods has a familiarity and a comfort level for many Jews, like me, who are only two generations away from the terror of the early twentieth century. I don't know the origins of brisket or pickled herring, but eating these foods reminds me of who I am. It provides a palpable connection to the past.

The very personal relationship we have to our culture's food accounts for why so many of us are reluctant to try foods from *other* cultures. Some foods break free from the confines of culture—bagels, burritos, and now sushi have been adopted by the larger consumer culture as their own. But it's the rarer tastes, the ones we don't innately know or appreciate, that require work. And Patty and I have done good work on this week of crossing cultures—I have sampled kimchi, she's sampled chopped liver. We are well on our way.

And here we are, with Stella, at the end of the road at Yonah Shimmel's Knishes right next door to Katz's. It is 8,000 degrees outside and not air-conditioned inside. A sign hangs underneath the counter: You Don't Have to Be Jewish to Eat a Knish.

"Stella," I say, "you have to have a knish." Stella, the vegetarian, hardly ate anything at Katz's.

"I dunno. What is it?"

"It's a potato ball thingie," I say, unhelpfully.

"Ummm."

I tell the woman at the counter that we want two. "One toasted garlic and onion," I say (that's the special knish of the day). "And which one do you want, Stella?"

"Spinach, I guess."

We sit at a table, Patty hot and full from her corned beef.

"So how did you like Jewish food?" I ask Patty.

"I liked it. It's not good for you, though, is it?"

"Ha!" I laugh. "Not really, no."

Then I think and add: "Well, chicken soup is good for you when you have a cold."

The knishes arrive. They are smoking hot, which is the last thing anyone wants on such a hot day. But we let them cool and order vanilla sodas in the meantime. When the knishes have cooled, we dig in and nod and consider.

"These are the best knishes in America," I say, pointing to an article on the wall. "People come from all over to have them."

Stella is enjoying hers.

"I like this," she says. "It tastes like when I was younger and I used to put mashed potatoes on my biscuits."

That connection—that mechanism for linking something exotic with something familiar—is precisely the sort of thing one requires to reach out and experience the new. The Korean barbecue was familiar enough—the beef, the lettuce, the green onions—to grant me access. That was the bridge from the private sanctum of my culture to the private sanctum of Patty's culture. Stella has hit the nail on the head and I must retract what I've said earlier.

"Stella," I declare, "I crown you the official mascot of the cross-cultures chapter."

She swallows a bit of knish and shrugs. "Eh," she says, like an old Jew.

I smile and laugh, as does Patty.

Stella is transformed—a knish has unlocked her inner Jew—and Patty and I are kvelling.

• • •

For those of you who want to unlock your inner Jew but who don't live near a Jewish deli, here's a recipe for chopped liver from America's premier authority on Jewish food, Joan Nathan, author of *Jewish Cooking in America*. The recipe is credited to retired lobbyist Hyman Bookbinder, whom, according to Nathan, everyone calls Bookie.

Bookie's Chopped Chicken Liver
From *Jewish Cooking in America*

Makes 10 to 12 servings as a predinner nosh or as an appetizer on a leaf of lettuce

4 large eggs
3 to 4 tablespoons vegetable oil
3 medium onions, diced
$1/4$ green pepper, seeded and diced (optional)
1 pound fresh chicken livers
Salt and freshly ground pepper
1 tablespoon chicken fat (optional)

1. Put the eggs in cold water in a saucepan. Bring to a boil and simmer for about 10 minutes. Cool rapidly in iced water and peel.

2. Heat the oil in a 10-inch skillet. Sauté the onions and green pepper over a high heat for about 5 minutes, until the onions start turning brown.

3. Add the chicken livers to the sautéed onions and green pepper and cook, tossing the livers occasionally, until they are firm, about 5 minutes. (Don't let them become tough by overcooking.)

4. Chop together the livers, hard-boiled eggs, sliced or quartered, and the sautéed onions and green pepper, using an old-fashioned manual chopper or food processor until of even consistency, but not pureed. Season with salt and pepper.

5. If you want, add a tablespoon of chicken fat to the mix.

FIVE

Fear Not the Knife

Eric "Bubba" Gabrynowycz loves his knife.

Eric is the sous chef at the Union Square Café in New York. At 8:15 on a Saturday morning, in the empty restaurant dining room, he shows off his chef's knife to me and my roommate/friend Diana.

"Your knife is like your baby in the kitchen," he declares. "I bought mine on my first day of culinary school and it goes everywhere in the world with me. I'd sleep with it if I could."

My friend Molly, who is a waitress at the Union Square Café, arranged this meeting for us. I am a mediocre knife person. I don't sharpen my knives, so they are dull and frequently difficult to cut with. My chopping technique is wobbly and unprofessional. It is high time that I learned the ways of the knife, the magic methodology behind knife usage and maintenance. And what better place to learn than at one of the city's most beloved and most revered restaurants?

I know this much going in: knives are to chefs what brushes are to painters, what pianos are to pianists. A chef is only as great as his or her knife. If there's one tool most chefs would want to have on a desert island it would almost certainly be a sharp knife.

Yet, there's a certain person in my life who is skeptical of this whole sharp-knife business. She believes that sharp knives are dangerous, that the hazards of keeping a sharp knife around are more troubling than the dangers of using a dull knife. That friend is Diana.

"So is this your assistant?" asks Eric as he lays out his knives on a cutting board, getting ready to demonstrate.

"Not really, no. I brought Diana because she's afraid of knives. She doesn't believe that bigger, sharper knives are safer than not-so-sharp knives."

Diana giggles and turns red. Her girlishness is a cloak that hides the sharp dagger that is her brain.

Eric swivels around and stares at Diana. "Are you kidding? A sharp knife is *completely* and *utterly* safer."

"I know, I know," stammers Diana, blushing a bit. "It's just that . . . well . . . you can't accidentally chop your finger off with a dull knife."

"Not true! Nothing is more dangerous than a big, dull, heavy knife," says Eric. He is speaking fast. "If a knife is sharp," he continues, "it'll do the work for you. If the knife does the work for you, it isn't dangerous."

He takes an onion and slices the top and bottom off, slices it in half, and peels off the skin.

"Watch this," he says. He places his left hand on the onion and curls up his fingers so that they create a wall against which the knife rests. And then, effortlessly, he glides the knife both down and across, slicing the onion perfectly.

"See," he says. "The knife is doing all the work."

Diana and I watch and then he calls Diana over. "Okay," he says. "Your turn."

Diana steps over to the table of knives and Eric asks Diana to hold the knife the way she normally holds a knife.

She nervously lifts the knife off the table and holds it by the handle.

"Okay," he says. "You don't want to hold it like that— you don't have control. You want to hold it like a pencil with your fingers on the blade."

He slides her hand up and has her pinch the top of the blade. "This way," he explains, "you have more control; it won't slip around."

Diana grips the top of the knife and Eric slides the onion over. "Now you want to slice down and pull through."

Diana moves the knife down and across and makes several efficient slices.

"Good," says Eric.

"How does it feel?" I ask her.

Diana pauses a moment and looks at me. "It feels good," she says. Yet her fear, manifested in a trembling hand and a deeply nervous look on her face, makes me wonder if she'll ever truly embrace the gospel of the big sharp knife.

A Quick Examination of Diana's Psychology

During lunch later that day with Diana and her older sister, Rachel, who's visiting from California, the two of them recount their parents' peculiar safety obsessions.

Both of their parents are doctors. Consequently, they are constantly concerned about their children's health and well-being.

"We weren't allowed to jump on trampolines when we were kids," says Diana, laughing. "We had to ride bicycles with a helmet . . . we couldn't eat fruit that wasn't grown in the U.S. All of our meat had to be well done."

"That's crazy," I say, trying to be nonjudgmental.

"If we went to a barbecue," says Rachel, "we couldn't eat anything that might've been touched by the person making the burgers. We weren't allowed to eat the potato chips."

The two of them, I detect, have rarely spoken about the overprotective environment in which they were raised: their energy gains as they speak.

"My youngest brother and I would sometimes sneak out to Burger King," says Diana, "because we weren't allowed to have fast food.

"And I remember once," she continues, "we went to our grandmother's house for dinner. She was shaking dressing in a jar with a rusty lid, so our mother whispered to us that we weren't allowed to have the salad. We all had to make up a reason not to eat it."

Rachel laughs and shakes her head.

I ask them both if they have completely outgrown their parents' neuroses or if they're neurotic about food and safety themselves.

"Well," confesses Rachel, "recently I bought a can of tomatoes and when I came home I saw that the can didn't have a date."

She lowers her head and laughs at herself. "So I went back to the store and bought another can just to be safe."

Diana titters with recognition. She would probably have done the same thing.

Fear in the kitchen is a significant impediment to growing as a chef.

Kitchen fear is a healthy mechanism: it's perfectly sensible to be slightly afraid when you flame your bananas Foster or when you deep-fry a batch of potatoes. There are risks involved with cooking, everyone knows this. Many adults avoid the kitchen because of scarring experiences from their childhood. The kitchen is a place where you can get hurt and many people don't think the danger is worth the reward. "Why burn my kitchen down when I can order Chinese?"

There is a scar on my left hand, right over my ring finger knuckle, from when I was six or seven and I burned my hand on the stove, making eggs with my mom. I remember the moment quite well: the way the pan was situated on the stove, the way I was standing on tiptoe to see what was happening, and the feeling of shock and terror when my hand somehow landed on the rim of the pan.

Alive in that moment was a synaptic process that accounts for most people's kitchen neuroses. The step between the burn and the crying out is the same step you probably see when a small child falls off a bicycle or off the monkey bars. Have you ever seen small children fall? They pause, reflect, and react. It's as if their brains are screaming out: "Oh, my God! Do you realize what just happened? I can't believe that happened! I better start crying now!"

When you compare that to how a chef reacts to pain, the difference is startling. On the Food Network alone, I've watched chefs stick their hands into boiling pots to taste sauces; I've seen them lift food out of searing hot pans directly from the oven using only their fingers. Mario Batali, my favorite TV chef, is the most brazen chef I've ever seen. He'll press raw meat into pots as they sizzle with spattering olive oil, his hand directly over the heat.

Compare that to Diana, who, when she was home for the holidays, made a chicken dish for her family that involved browning the chicken.

"My mom came in and saw the chicken spattering," she recalls, "and she told me to put on a pair of *goggles*."

How does Diana, a self-described foodie, reconcile her fear-laden past with a lifestyle that requires utter fearlessness?

For that matter, how do I reconcile my own nervousness

and my own nervous upbringing with the challenges of the kitchen?

I come from a mother who sent me anti-radiation medicine and Cipro after 9/11, who thinks I should never ride the subway because it's too dangerous (she wants me to take cabs everywhere). As a child, I'd go to amusement parks and my mom would stop the ride for me if it was too scary. We have a video of us at Nunley's, the now-defunct Long Island amusement park, and I'm on the mini-kiddie roller coaster and I'm yelling, "Stop the ride!" and Mom's yelling at the operator to switch it off. That's just a small taste of my nervous upbringing.

How did I get from there to the point where I am now? I'm pretty fearless in the kitchen. I fry things on a whim, I light things on fire. Is this a reaction formation, am I rebelling against my own upbringing? Or is the kitchen a fortress of solitude, a psychological cocoon, where I can overcome my lifelong fears and neuroses?

Maybe.

But then you look at Eric "Bubba" Gabrynowycz as he wields his kitchen knives and you realize he's of a different breed. His handshake is super strong, his energy is manly and athletic. He's even wearing a baseball cap.

I'm terrified of baseball. Not just playing baseball but watching the game. I'm always scared the ball's going to come flying into the bleachers and hit me in the head.

Maybe that's why the kitchen is such a wonderful place: it's a great equalizer. Great chefs and minor chefs are all working with the same basic equipment and resources. Sharp things and fire—these are the basic tools required.

And how you wield those tools, whether you do so with quivering fear or bold fearlessness, determines how well you will do. Because if one thing is true about cooking it is this: the meek shall not inherit anything in the kitchen.

Eric draws a V in my notepad.

"This is what you want your knife to look like," he explains. "You want it to come together like a V." He scribbles and shows how most knives look before they are sharpened.

"You sharpen it to get it back to the V shape." He draws the V sharper. "Sharpening a knife is an art. You can spend five minutes doing it, you can spend thirty minutes doing it."

He removes a whetstone from a tub of water, then takes his knife and begins to slide it across the stone in a motion that looks like carefully practiced choreography.

"Your knife will last forever if you take care of it, if you treat it well."

Asking a chef about his knives is like asking a new mother about her baby or asking a novelist about his newest book. It's something a chef loves to talk about.

"You have to tell your readers how to chop herbs," he says. "I'm going to get some basil."

He exits to the kitchen and returns a few moments later with a bunch of basil.

"You have to have a sharp knife when you cut herbs. Most people cut down like a guillotine and they bruise the herbs. Do you ever notice how the outside of basil turns black after you cut it?"

I nod and he says, "That's because you've bruised it, you haven't cut it the right way."

He lays the basil flat and glides the tip of the knife across, delicately slicing the basil.

"Use the whole knife: use the blade almost like with meat. Glide it across, don't chop down."

He shows us his work and we both smile our approval.

"So do you ever take your knives in to get sharpened or do you always sharpen them yourself?"

Eric looks at me as if he's about to share a secret.

"Well, usually I do it myself. But," and then he pauses and crosses his arms, "if a knife is very special, if I really love a knife, I'll go to Korin."

There's a hush in the room and a breeze blows mysteriously across our brows.

"Korin?" I ask.

"Yes, Korin. It's in TriBeCa. It's where all the chefs go."

I write down the name and ask a few more questions about knives and cutting boards (Eric is firmly against bamboo: he thinks it damages the blade) and then Diana and I say our thank-yous and make our way out into the bright morning air.

● ● ●

An hour later we are at Korin in TriBeCa. The window display features a samurai warrior. Diana and I are the furthest things from samurai warriors: we're samurai wimps. A sign says Ring Doorbell to Enter. Diana presses the button, the door buzzes, and we enter.

The space is small and hot, and all we see are shelves with rice cookers, Japanese serving dishes, and—up high, near the ceiling—samurai swords.

"Hello," says a voice from the back.

Diana and I walk deeper into the store and see two women behind a desk.

"How can we help you?" asks one of the women.

Diana specifically told me before we entered that she wasn't going to buy a knife today, that she'd merely look.

"Well," I say, "I'm working on a book about food and I'm doing a chapter on knives. What can you tell us about knives?"

The woman stares at me.

"Also, my friend Diana here is looking for a knife."

Diana shoots me a look but I ignore it.

"What kind of knife are you looking for?"

"A chef's knife," I say, when Diana says nothing. "Just a basic knife for chopping."

The woman leads us to a glass case filled with Japanese knives. "These are Misono. They're very good."

"That one looks nice," I say, pointing to a large chef's knife. The woman removes it and hands it to Diana, who takes it with her left hand.

"Oh, are you a lefty?"

Diana nods.

"Then we have a better knife for you."

She goes to another cabinet and removes a shiny chef's knife that she hands to Diana. "How does it feel?"

Diana grins. "Wow, I didn't even know they made left-handed knives."

"The knife master is here today—he will sharpen it for you if you buy it."

"The knife master?" I ask.

And just then, a smiling man enters in jean shorts with gray hair parted down the middle. He walks past us and goes up a set of stairs.

"That," says the woman, looking after him, "is the knife master."

Diana buys the knife—the spirit of Korin has won her over.

In my backpack are my two chef's knives wrapped in kitchen towels: the Calphalon knife that came with my knife set and a Wüsthof knife that I bought a few years earlier. When the knife master is ready to see us, we present him with four knives: the two from my backpack, the one Diana has just purchased, and a Misono that I buy on impulse—because I don't have any Japanese knives. It is now, incidentally, my favorite knife.

The knife master smiles at us as he sits in a wicker chair and begins the knife-sharpening ritual. He lays a cloth on his lap and lifts a basin of water onto the stool in front of him. He sees me taking notes as he does all this and says, "You writer?"

"Yes," I say and he nods seriously. Perhaps I have commanded his respect the way he has commanded mine.

He lifts the Calphalon chef's knife and studies it, then shakes his head back and forth and calls me over.

"Look."

Diana and I go closer and look.

"Broken," he says and points to a chip on the knife's surface that I'd never noticed before.

"Oh, no," I say, genuinely surprised. I didn't realize I'd been chopping with a chipped knife.

"You might as well not sharpen it—I guess it's no good."

The words don't really register for him. He rises from his seat and says, "Come. You want to see?"

We both nod, not really sure what we're going to see. He leads us away from the knife-sharpening station and toward a hallway in the back. The hallway leads to a flight of stairs that go down into a basement stacked with papers, files, and cabinets.

He leads us past a desk with a fax machine and a computer (Korin, apparently, sharpens knives for many of the city's top chefs, including Jean-Georges and Eric Ripert), past two men repairing the bathroom floor, over to a corner with three bright, colorful machines.

"Repair," he says as he sits at a neon green machine with a large wheel.

He lifts an ancient bucket that is filled with water. In the bucket floats a golden ladle.

"Watch," he commands as he starts the wheel. As it spins rapidly, he takes a rag, dips it in the bucket, and wets the wheel. Then, with a dramatic flourish, he takes my chipped knife to the spinning surface. The sound is piercing.

A mere moment or two later, the wheel has stopped and he holds up the knife. "Fixed," he says, and Diana and I go to examine. The chip is gone.

"Now we make finer."

He turns the wheel on again, wets it with the rag, and holds the knife to it. His motions are balletic, much like Eric's at the Union Square Café. These knife-sharpening rituals are truly ancient—there's a religiosity to this whole process that makes Diana and me feel that we are witnessing a spiritual event.

This is particularly true when we are back upstairs, my Calphalon knife restored, when the knife master sees to the three other knives.

At first, he uses a whetstone the way that Eric did at Union Square. But then he lifts a stone out of a box on the floor. The stone is deep gray: "Very rare stone," whispers the knife man. "Costs three thousand dollars."

He places the stone on the work surface in front of him and then places each of our knives, one by one, on its surface, coaxing the knives across like a true artist, a man deeply connected to what he is doing.

He does this with each knife and then he removes another stone. "This one four thousand dollars."

And again, he puts our knives to the stone and we are

completely captivated. Even Diana, who began this day wary of sharp knives, is in awe of what she is witnessing.

"It's amazing," she says as he performs his task.

Then, the knife sharpening complete, the knife master (whose name, I later learned, is Chiharu Sugai) stands and removes a piece of newspaper from a stack. He holds the paper, lifts Diana's knife to it, and as he slices down the paper splits perfectly in half.

He smiles broadly. "Very sharp. Is good?"

"It's great," I say and watch him do the same with the three other knives. When he finishes he bows and goes upstairs.

"Thank you so much," I say over and over again.

When we go to the register to pay, the woman there declares, "Today's your lucky day. It's normally fifteen dollars minimum per knife for sharpening, plus the repair." I begin to do the math in my head.

"But," she says respectfully, "he says not to charge you."

Diana and I shake our heads disbelievingly.

She wraps up our knives and puts them in a bag. We leave the store, equipped with sharp knives—my old ones restored—and Diana, the knife fearer, is suddenly in possession of a knife sharpened and sanctified by a knife master.

At my apartment late that afternoon, I am slicing newspaper like it's my job.

"Watch!" I say to my audience of Diana, Rachel, and my boyfriend, Craig.

I flip pages of the *New York Times* open and slide my Misono knife down the page so the paper splits perfectly in two like the knife master did.

"Isn't that cool? Look how sharp this is!"

My audience looks back at me, bored, and I say to Diana, "Take out your knife. Let's go slice a peach."

In my kitchen is a peach purchased the day before from the farmer's market. We place it on a cutting board and I begin with my knife, laying the blade on the top of the fruit and allowing its sharpness to fall through the flesh, much like Eric said it should earlier that day.

"Now you try," I say to Diana, who wields her knife cautiously.

She approaches the peach, lifts her knife with her left hand, and lowers the precious blade onto the fruit, which absorbs the knife as if this cutting were a cosmic event just waiting to happen.

"It's so smooth. It really does make a difference."

We stand transfixed, watching pieces of peach fall away, both of us now completely aware of the majesty and importance of this essential kitchen tool.

SIX

Cook for a Date

"Mission successful, man."

I hear these words on my voice mail at 12:24 a.m., late Tuesday night. The voice is my friend Kirk's, and the mission is of my devising.

Some missions are noble missions: rescue a soldier, evacuate a building. Others are less so. Noble or not, this mission is one that relates to this very chapter—"Cook for a Date." It may be subtitled: "Mission: Seduction." Or: "Mission: Get the Religious Mormon Girl to Kiss Kirk." Ours is a mission that many people find themselves on at various points in their lives. It is a mission to express love, affection, or desire with food, and to get some back in return.

It's the sort of mission that justifies learning to cook. In fact, if you don't buy the psychological mumbo-jumbo I've espoused in previous chapters—the whole free-your-soul-through-cooking concept—then allow me to offer an alternate incentive: cooking gets you laid.

Cooking is a sensual act: it requires sensitivity. You dip your finger in to taste the sauce and in doing so you feel heat, you feel texture; various aromas waft toward your nose as you bring the liquid to your lips and taste. There's warmth and moisture; there's fire, there's chill. Cooking is like sex without the hassle; it's engaged passion with a tangible reward.

Kirk calls me the day before his date to discuss logistics. Dee (not her real name), a Mormon, has gone out with Kirk many times, but they've never kissed.

"She's really religious," he says. "And she doesn't drink."

Kirk himself is what he calls "post-Mormon." He grew up in the Mormon church, a church that places premarital sex a notch below murder on the scale of sin. Because of his Mormon background, Kirk isn't unfamiliar with the concept of a mission: he spent three years of his life doing missionary work in Siberia.

"I learned to cook for myself in Russia," he tells me as I plan his menu. "I'm actually not that bad in the kitchen."

When in Russia, Kirk knocked on doors and espoused the merits of Mormonism. In the process he was beaten up quite regularly; at one point, his roommate on the trip was pierced by a scythe. My mission is a little less dangerous.

For this mission, I want to choose foods that are special yet easy to cook in Kirk's small, un-air-conditioned New York apartment kitchen. More important, I want to pick foods that are sensual, sexy, and guaranteed to win a girl's heart.

"Believe me, we'll get her to kiss you," I assure him. "I'm a culinary Cupid and you're about to score."

I scored myself a few weeks earlier, cooking for my own date. Craig and I had been going out for a few weeks when I finally delivered to him a much-sought-after, much-anticipated home-cooked meal.

"When are you going to cook for me?" he would ask persistently. These are the perils of making yourself known as a person who cooks.

There are two schools of thought regarding how to approach cooking for a date when you've made yourself known as a person who cooks. The first is the "cook what you know" school. Make something simple, straightforward, and satisfying—a bowl of pasta, a roast chicken. This is the strategy of someone who wants to appear elegant, sophisticated, and clearly at ease in the kitchen.

The other school is the one I matriculated in when I set out to cook Craig dinner. It is the school of hyperambition, of shooting for the culinary moon—to put it bluntly, overdoing it. A good cook, like a good dancer, makes his art appear effortless. Watch Gene Kelly splashing through puddles in *Singin' in the Rain*. His grace, his pluck, is a function of his craft: he knows what he's doing and he makes his complicated dancing look like child's play.

And then there's me cooking from Suzanne Goin's

beautiful, yet incredibly challenging, *Sunday Suppers at Lucques.* The dish is Deviled Chicken Thighs on Braised Leeks. When Craig rings the doorbell, the chicken is sizzling loudly in a pan of hot oil, the leeks are gurgling in the oven, and the bread crumbs are toasting in butter that may be a little too brown.

"Hey!" I say frantically as I pull the door open.

"Hey," says Craig calmly, putting his arms around me. I quickly pull free. "Can't . . . talk . . . have . . . to . . . cook."

Craig watches me return to the kitchen, a concerned look on his face.

"Wow," he says, surveying the scene. "Look at all this."

I nod and smile and flip the chicken, shake the bread crumbs, and check on the leeks.

"I just came from school," he says. "I was editing that movie for—"

"Can you go away?" I say quite suddenly.

Craig looks shocked.

"I mean," I recover. "Can you go into the other room? I'm sorry . . . it's just, I'm a little overwhelmed."

Craig smiles and kisses me on the head. "Okay," he says. "I'll check my e-mail."

He walks into the bedroom, closes the door, and I am at peace. Or am I? What's the purpose of this meal? Is it seduction or alienation? Craig exiled to the bedroom and I'm placing chicken thighs onto a bed of leeks, rubbing them with a mustard mixture, and topping them with brown-butter bread crumbs.

Who am I doing this for: him or me?

• • •

Kirk's menu is edgy because it's not seasonal, it's purely sensual. It starts with fennel Parmesan salad, moves to a wild mushroom risotto, and climaxes—oh, yes, climaxes—with chocolate mousse. This is my seduction strategy, the Xs and Os on the chalkboard before the big football game.

At Kirk's apartment, we unpack the groceries and I survey the scene. The living room is neat enough, but his roommates bustle in and out. The kitchen has a puddle on the floor and the mixing bowls are dirty.

"I think I'll put the table in my bedroom," says Kirk, "'cause there's an air conditioner in there and my roommates won't be buzzing by."

Normally I'd say such a move was presumptuous, but considering the current circumstances, it's the right way to go.

"First," I say, "let's make the chocolate mousse. That needs time to refrigerate."

Chocolate mousse is an obvious choice for a romantic dessert. Most women I know quiver at the mention of chocolate. Add to that two of the most overtly sexual ingredients known—cream and eggs, the basic formula for reproduction—and you have a dessert more sexed up than Venus emerging from her clamshell.

"Let me do that," says Kirk as I begin to crack the eggs. "This is *my* romantic dinner, remember?"

Kirk is absolutely right: the first rule of cooking a romantic dinner is that the amount of love you put into the food yourself is directly proportional to the amount of love you get in return. I need to keep my love out of his mousse.

Chocolate Mousse

From *Chez Panisse Desserts,* by Lindsey R. Shere

Makes 3 ¾ cups

5 ounces semisweet chocolate, chopped
1 ounce unsweetened chocolate, chopped
2 tablespoons brandy or Cognac
2 tablespoons brewed coffee or water
4 eggs, separated
1 cup whipping cream

Melt the chocolate with the brandy and coffee in a small heavy saucepan over warm water, or in a double boiler. Stir until well melted, smooth, and glossy. Remove the chocolate from the heat. Whisk the egg yolks into the chocolate mixture. Whip the cream until it holds a very soft shape. In a heat-proof bowl, swirl the egg whites above a gas flame or over hot water until they are barely warm. Beat them until they hold very soft peaks and fold about a quarter of them into the chocolate mixture. Fold in the remaining whites, then fold in the whipped cream. Pour into serving glasses or a serving bowl, cover with plastic wrap, and chill until firm.

Serve with whipped cream.

"Do you have any brandy or Cognac?" I ask.

"Dee doesn't drink, remember?" says Kirk.

"Oh, yeah," I say.

There's a pause.

"I mean," I say, "if we put some in there, do you think she'd notice?"

Kirk is quiet.

"It's not like we're slipping her a roofie," I argue. "It's part of the recipe."

"We don't have any here," he says, "but they might have some upstairs."

He quickly exits and returns with a bottle of rum.

"Does rum work?" he asks.

"I think it does," I say as I unscrew the lid.

Whether we poured any in and how much we poured in—if we poured any in—is the sort of secret a chef never reveals, even to his reading public.

Craig loves the chicken thighs.

"These are amazing," he says as he carves indulgently through the bread crumbs, the chicken meat, the leeks. "You are so talented," he cheers. "I totally won the lottery."

These are the things a young cook wants to hear, especially on a date. But I am exhausted: the cooking left me hollowed out, severely fatigued.

"There's bread pudding in the oven," I say robotically. "It has bread, butter, cream, chocolate . . ."

"Yum," says Craig, cutting himself another piece of chicken. "You're such a good cook."

Am I? Is a good cook so tired after cooking such a big meal? Does a good cook exhaust himself the way I've exhausted myself, without brain power for conversation or any other kind of discourse?

This, I discover, is the second rule for cooking for a date: don't leave yourself drained. Make it easy on yourself so you're there to enjoy it when the food is done.

Which is a nice segue to a meal, several weeks later, that is completely spontaneous and much more fun. At the farmer's market, ramps, or "wild leeks," are in season. I've never purchased ramps but I am there with Craig, we're walking through, and I buy ramps and green garlic. Back home, I put water on to boil and get out my sauté pan and my cutting board. Following a recipe I find online, I slice the ramps thinly and the garlic too. When the water boils, I add salt and spaghetti. I heat olive oil in the sauté pan, then add the ramps, garlic, and crushed red pepper. I sauté it till it's lightly colored, then splash in some pasta cooking water (white wine would work too), let it cook down, then add the spaghetti just before it's done. I cook them together, twirl it with tongs onto two separate plates, and grate tons of cheese on top. I serve two glasses of chilled white wine and Craig is a happy man.

"I like cooking for you," I say as I watch him slurp his spaghetti.

"I like you cooking for me too," he says, mouth full, a happy look on his face.

The dinner, while not particularly lusty or overtly sexual, is perfectly romantic. I am there eating with my date and we may as well be on the moon.

The mousse is done and now Kirk and I are prepping the fennel salad. Because the main course is wild mushroom risotto, and because risotto and chocolate mousse are both very rich, I want something light and refreshing to go with it. A salad is a perfect choice, and nothing could be simpler than sliced fennel, lemon, and Parmesan. Perhaps the crispness of the fennel will add a snap to the evening, the lemon a brightness, and the Parmesan a musky, husky wallop of flavor. The basic components of a simple salad may be the very ones that set two young hearts alight, the unconscious motivators that lead to a lifetime of happiness and convivial cohabitation.

Raw Fennel and Parmesan Salad
From *Italian Easy (Recipes from The River Cafe)*,
by Rose Gray and Ruth Rogers

2 fennel bulbs
3 tablespoons lemon juice
4 tablespoons extra-virgin olive oil
2 ounces Parmesan
6 prosciutto or salami slices

Trim the fennel. Chop the leafy tops and set aside. Slice the bulbs lengthwise very thinly and toss together with the lemon juice and olive oil, then season with salt and pepper to taste. Shave the Parmesan and combine. Marinate for 1 hour, tossing occasionally. Before serving, add the fennel tops. Serve with prosciutto.

Cooking is an exercise in communication: the ingredients communicate their freshness, the recipes communicate their patented formulas, the pans communicate their readiness, and the dish itself communicates the passion of the chef. What you place down before a loved one is itself a meaningful gesture, a symbol of your feelings as reflected in the portion size, the placement on the plate, and the thing itself. What did you cook? Did you microwave a hot dog or did you roast a quail? Did you microwave the hot dog with love and roast the quail with indifference? These things matter.

To communicate with maximum force you must cook with maximum feeling. What you make should be something you love yourself, a dish you can get excited about. This holds true for most things in life. Would a fifth-grader rather write a book report about *Crime and Punishment* or *Harry Potter*? Would you rather read this book or the phone book? (Please don't answer that question!)

Because cooking is a form of communication, there are

two sides to the equation: the deliverer of the message and the receiver, the one doing the cooking and the one being cooked for. You can cook with all the passion in your soul, but if the second half of the equation isn't in the mood for food, isn't in the mood for you, really, there's little you can do to promote sparkage. To rephrase: you must know your audience. That's the third and final rule of cooking for a date.

There was a time, in fact, that I was on the receiving end of a romantic meal that I didn't want. He was a very sweet guy, I met him through friends, and I liked him enough to go out a few times. But then Valentine's Day rolled around and he wanted to cook me a Valentine's Day breakfast. This disturbed me.

"I'm nervous," I told him. "I don't want you to put yourself out."

"I'm not putting myself out!" he cheered. And then he spent forty dollars on ingredients, woke up at 6 a.m., and cooked for three hours. I've never eaten a guiltier meal in my life.

Cooking is a tool of seduction, true, but it's also a tool of entrapment. Make sure the person you're cooking for wants to be cooked for; that what you're cooking is something that he or she wants to eat.

Wild mushroom risotto is a dish that we hope Dee will like. If not, there's always the philosophy that cooking a heartfelt meal for somebody is a weeding-out process. If she doesn't like your wild mushroom risotto, why in the world would you want to date her? Especially when you spent an hour in an un-air-conditioned kitchen stirring constantly over a hot stove? Especially when the wild mushrooms cost fifteen dollars.

"She better like it," I say as I unpack the wild mushrooms.

I paid for the wild mushrooms.

Wild Mushroom Risotto
From *The Chez Panisse Cookbook*, by Paul Bertolli with Alice Waters

Serves 4

4 to 6 cups raw wild mushrooms (chanterelles, horns of plenty, dentinum, boletes, etc.)
8 tablespoons unsalted butter
Salt and pepper
2 shallots (2 ounces), finely diced
1 1/2 cups Arborio rice
2 ounces pancetta, diced
1 cup dry white wine
1 1/2 quarts simmering chicken broth
1 tablespoon chopped fresh Italian parsley
1 teaspoon chopped fresh thyme

Brush off any dirt from the mushrooms with a small vegetable brush. Use a knife to cut away any implanted dirt. Slice the mushrooms. Melt 2 tablespoons of the butter in a sauté pan, add the mushrooms, salt, and pepper, and cook for 8 to 15 minutes (this depends on how much moisture they contain) until nearly all of the liquid they release has evaporated. You should end up with approximately 2 cups mushrooms. Set aside.

Melt 2 more tablespoons of the butter in a 6-quart noncorroding pot. Add the shallots and let them soften over medium heat for 2 minutes. Add the rice and the pancetta and cook for 3 minutes, stirring often. Do not allow the rice to brown. Stir in the wine and allow it to nearly evaporate. Then begin making the broth additions. Add only enough broth to maintain the liquid level just above the rice. Maintain a gentle simmer and add broth when the level begins to drop, but before the previously added amount has been entirely absorbed. Stir the rice often, before and after each addition.

After 15 minutes, raise the heat and add the mushrooms. Readjust the heat so that the rice simmers. Cook for about 5 minutes more. During the final cooking, make broth additions judiciously and taste the rice frequently to gauge its progress. When it is nearly done (chewy but not firm in the center), stir in the remaining 4 tablespoons butter and make any final corrections to salt and pepper. The risotto should be unified so that the sauce does not separate from the rice, but should not be so reduced that the rice becomes thick. The consistency should be nearly pourable. Stir in the fresh herbs and serve in warm bowls.

When I leave, the shallots are diced, the thyme is pulled off the stems, and the mushrooms are cooked. "Mmmm," says Kirk, tasting a mushroom. "These are awesome."

A pot is set out with the chicken stock and another set out for cooking the risotto.

"You understand the process? You get the chicken stock simmering and then you add it to the rice a little at a time until it's all absorbed."

"Yes. I get it."

I survey the scene. The chocolate mousse is in the refrigerator, the fennel salad is marinating in a bowl. The risotto ingredients are all laid out, a perfect mise en place. The dinner is like a row of fireworks waiting for a single match.

"Okay, I think you're all set."

I put my knife and salt and pepper back in the suitcase I wheeled to Kirk's. (I brought pots and pans just in case his weren't good.) I study the bowls and plates and suggest which ones to serve the dinner in.

"I think I'm good. I'm going to go rest before she comes over."

And so, with a final "Good luck," I'm out the door.

On my way home, I wonder if this is really a decent exercise in cooking for a date. After all, the impetus for it all is me. I'm the one who got the ball rolling. Does that take away from the romance, if it wasn't instigated by Kirk?

And what about the food itself? I picked it, not Kirk, so

how authentic can his passion be? How much love will be transferred?

All these concerns are assuaged, though, later that night—at 12:24 a.m.—when Kirk leaves his message. "Mission successful, man."

I later urge him to write me a detailed account of how it all went down—how the cooking transpired, how she reacted. Here's what happened after I left, written by Kirk in an e-mail:

All right, man, here it goes.

After you left I had about an hour and a half to do an hour's worth of work. Unfortunately for everyone involved, South Park *was on.*

So now I had an hour to do an hour's worth of work in the kitchen while also getting super sexxified for my date. I grabbed an unwilling roommate and made him stand there while I read him the entire set of directions twice (I really did this). After I heard it out loud it looked less like words just swimming all over the page (a sensation due in equal parts to my dyslexia and the fact that I had dropped the directions in chicken stock).

The salad was taken care of and the mousse just needed a little freshly whipped cream. I had planned to put off whipping the cream till she got there, because I thought if she got to help it would make her feel like a part of the process and also help her realize how hard it is to whip things, thus giving me a few points on the effort meter. But the risotto still had a long way to go, so I took a shower 'cause I needed to shave, then got right down to cooking.

The thing that was the most troublesome to me was maintaining the chicken stock level in the pot. The tricky phrase was "Maintain a gentle simmer and add broth when the level begins to drop, but before the previously added amount has been entirely absorbed." This was okay when I first poured it in, but the more things got asimmering the more this started to feel like a pretty broad judgment call by yours truly.

Not to mention I was having to make other judgment calls, such as shirt choice (an old button-up that I felt was simultaneously classy and carefree) and dining music (a band called Hot Chip, which is a nice mellow British band playing their songs to some seriously sweet hip-hop beats). I also had to set the table.

It was at this moment that Dee showed up. When she saw what was going on in the kitchen I could see her eyes fill up with lust and desire. I pulled a pot from the freezer and asked her if she wouldn't mind using a whisk to whip some cream for the chocolate mousse! *while I worked on the* wild mushroom risotto! *(BTW, my whipped cream plan came off perfectly. When her arm cramped up I could tell she appreciated my efforts that much more.)*

Then it was the moment of truth. I served the

risotto in some bowls and the salad on plates and we sipped grape juice to the soothing sounds of Hot Chip all evening. The food was (and I will go ahead and toot my own horn here) delish.

The recipe said to add salt, but I found that it was already plenty salty while not so salty as to overpower the mushrooms and herbs. All my fears about not adding stock at the right rate were absorbed into each succulent bite. The salad was fresh and simple, a nice palate cleanser. The mousse was rich and creamy to the point that after about seven bites we both felt like we would never stand upright again. The conversation went swimmingly.

Later on, while watching the movie Delicatessen, *I leaned over, still smelling of the sweet aromas from the kitchen, and planted a gentle kiss on her. She was so surprised that she actually yelled. Just a little.*

Not the food's fault; I just hadn't done a very good lead-up. But once she got over her initial shock, she got into it. Oh, yeah. My feet were planted firmly on first base that night!

You know, even though she dumped me a week later, I really do have to give the meal a lot of credit. Not so much for getting her in the mood, but for giving me the confidence to be able to make a move on this girl. Thank you, Adam. Thank you.

Sincerely,

Kirk

Love is complicated.

When I was younger, on Valentine's Day, my mother gave me a chocolate rose to give to Adrian, the girl who lived across the street. I crossed that street nervously, terrified of what she might say, and walked up the three steps that led to her door, knowing my mom was watching from inside our vestibule. Then I rang the doorbell, my palms sweaty, and waited for Adrian to come to the door.

She didn't come to the door—her older sister did.

"Is Adrian home?" I asked.

"No," said her sister, cracking gum.

"Oh," I said, bending the plastic end of the rose that was shaking ever so slightly in my hand.

"Can you give her this?" I asked, handing her the chocolate rose.

"Umm . . . okay," she said.

The door closed. I returned home.

"Well?" asked my mother.

"She wasn't home," I said. "I gave it to her sister."

That was that. I saw Adrian in school the next day and she didn't say anything. It was as if nothing happened: for all I knew that chocolate rose was snaking its way through Adrian's sister's digestive system, never to reach its intended destination.

And where that chocolate rose ended up is where most of our romantic efforts end up. Love is a tricky business. For those of us lucky enough to find someone whom we can cook for, those of us who find the right audience—

nothing is more intimate, more enlivening than feeding the person you love.

Or, for that matter, feeding the person you want to make out with.

Either way, the rewards are plentiful.

SEVEN

Cook for Your Family

This chapter is about cooking for your family. It's about food and love and how the two come together at the family table to forge feelings of fellowship and camaraderie, how food brings us together. Only, for me, there's a slight problem, a problem that makes this chapter difficult to write: my family won't let me cook for them!

My family is a restaurant family. My mom, as we learned in the first chapter, is a lively woman who likes eating out. She likes it so much that our kitchen is used mostly for storage, not cooking. The idea of me cooking dinner is anathema to my family's way of life.

I spent my childhood eating out at restaurants—every night a different place. Some nights it was a chain restaurant, other nights it was something local—usually with an early bird special. My childhood food memories are restaurant food memories: the spicy Cajun chicken pasta at T.G.I. Friday's, the limitless bread and salad at the Olive Garden, the fajitas at Chili's—these are the foods on which I was reared. My mother doesn't have any recipes of her own, but she staggered our weekly restaurant visits like a master. And my grandmother's recipe for restaurant lemonade is classic: one glass tap water, one packet Sweet'n Low, and the juice from several lemon wedges. Combine ingredients and stir. Taste for balance. Adjust accordingly.

These memories, as I ponder them, are as warm to me as any home-cooked meal. Some mothers and grandmothers use the stove and the oven as their instruments of nurture; my mother and grandmother used the telephone, the automobile, the menu, and the waitress. I felt well cared for. The energy my mother and grandmother spent on choosing where we would eat equals the energy most mothers and grandmothers spend on cooking dinner. Even to this day, when I come home, a thousand phone calls take place regarding where we will eat. "The first night we're going to Nick's, unless you want to go to Miami. But Dad doesn't come home from work until six." And when I agree to Nick's she'll call back an hour later and say, "You know, Hedy went to Nick's recently and hated it. Maybe we should go to Mario's."

The nexus of food, comfort, and care that usually takes place at the kitchen table is transferable in my family from restaurant to restaurant. Mom still represents the barrier between food and the stomachs of her children. "Don't eat that," my mom will say, "it doesn't look cooked." My grandmother will send things back if they're not to her liking, even if it's what you ordered. "Stop eating! We'll get you a new one!" It doesn't matter if they prepared the food themselves as long as they get to play lifeguard for what you let swim into your body.

If my life hadn't taken me in the direction that it's taken me, if food were just a means of sustenance and not an enduring passion, I think I could tolerate my family's eating habits the way I tolerate their TV-watching habits. (They Tivo *Regis and Kelly* and watch it at night. Now I Tivo *The View* and watch it at night too—what a thing to inherit!) I understand that my parents are social creatures and that they derive much pleasure from seeing their friends at their favorite restaurants. Most of my mom's friends aren't that different from her—they too populate the restaurants of Boca Raton on weeknights, consuming professionally prepared food on plates they won't have to wash themselves. It's a function of where they live and a lifetime of repetition that makes it less and less likely that my parents will ever truly enjoy the comforts of a home-cooked meal.

I just wish I didn't know what they were missing. Ever since I started cooking, my favorite meals have been the ones I've cooked for myself and my friends. No other meal can compare to a perfect roast chicken, stuffed with thyme and sprinkled with fennel seeds, cayenne pepper, salt, and pepper (Chez Panisse's recipe—use the best chicken you can find, approximately four pounds, and roast for one hour at 400 degrees). Serve with potatoes and apple cobbler for dessert, and there isn't a restaurant in existence that can do better. It pleases on a level that's almost primal: it reeks of goodness and comfort and *home*.

Or soup on a cold winter night. Or tomatoes in summer. Or brownies when you're depressed or apple pie when you're euphoric. These are the magic pathways to happiness I have discovered since leaving home. It's like my adult life is a forest and the restaurant bread crumbs I left home with ran out and were replaced with those I learned to make for myself. Now I want to share those bread crumbs with my family and they won't let me.

Seriously! They say no. For example, I'm going home for Mother's Day, so I call my mom to ask if I can cook a big Mother's Day dinner.

"No."

"What do you mean no?"

"No," she repeats. "We have reservations. I made them a few weeks ago."

"But it's for my book," I insist.

"I'm sorry. I don't want a big kadilla." (Kadilla is Yiddish for "ordeal.") "Can't you cook us lunch?"

Lunch? Lunch is barely worth the effort. What would I make for lunch? A salad? I know what she's doing here. She's trying to appease me by avoiding the real issue: sacrificing a well-loved restaurant meal for a genuine home-cooked one.

I decide to bring out the big guns.

"Michael can help." This is a power play. My mother always wants me and my brother to spend more time together, and cooking a big meal is certainly an opportunity for fostering brotherly camaraderie. This can't be denied. Plus Tali, my brother's girlfriend, can help too.

"I don't know," she sighs. "Who's going to clean it up?"

My mother's biggest gripe with cooking is the cleanup. What's the point of cooking if you have to clean it all up?

"I'll clean it up. I promise."

And then the unthinkable happens. The room begins to shake, dust cascades down from the furniture.

"Okay," says my mother. "I'll cancel the reservation."

I am speechless. Did she really say what I think she just said?

"Really?" I squeak.

"Yes," she answers. "What are you going to make?"

Her question rattles me out of my surprised stupor.

"Don't worry. It'll be something everyone will like."

I've done it! She's agreed to let me cook for her! It's a tremendous feat. It's so tremendous that I'm suddenly terrified: what will I cook?

I bet most of my readers worry over this same issue when dealing with their own families. Every family is like a government with varying immigration policies regarding the food they put in their stomachs. Some families have liberal immigration policies—they let in Mexican food, they let in Indian food, they let in Indonesian food—others, as we learned in the "Cross Cultures" chapter, have clearly defined borders and strict rules. These are the families that are difficult to cook for. They like their beef medium well. They like their mashed potatoes from a box, thank you very much. No fancy potatoes for us, please.

My family has an idiosyncratic immigration policy. They let some things in and leave others out. My dad's stomach politics are more conservative than my mother's. My dad likes what he likes. Once, when Craig asked my dad what he thought of as the perfect meal he answered, without a pause: "shrimp cocktail, Caesar salad, filet mignon cooked medium, onion rings, and banana cream pie." Incidentally, this is very close to the meal he eats every week at his favorite steakhouse. My mom likes the basics too—meat, chicken, fish. But she also likes more exotic fare. I remember going with her to Chinese restaurants when I was younger, and she'd order shrimp in lobster sauce, which impressed me to no end. I feel deep inside her is an adventurous eater. Unfortunately, this adventurous side is limited by whatever diet she and my grandmother are on at the time.

So I call home again, to discuss the dinner plan.

"I thought I'd make pasta."

"Your grandmother won't eat pasta."

Of course: pasta has carbs and carbs are out of vogue these days.

"Why don't you make something healthy? Like fish."

"I don't want to make fish." Fish bores me. I want to dazzle my family, I don't want to leave them shrugging their shoulders.

"What about chicken?" asks my mom. "You could make boneless, skinless—"

"Yes!" I suddenly say. "I'm going to make chicken: chicken with forty cloves of garlic."

"Is it skinless?"

"No," I cheer. "There's lots of skin. That's what makes it taste good."

A pause.

"And garlic," I add. "Lots of garlic."

My family loves garlic. If anyone in my family is hesitant to try something new—if, say, you order boar liver at dinner and everyone scoffs and scolds and says, "How could you eat boar liver? It's horrible!"—you can win them back over by telling them that there's garlic in it. Then they'll nibble, they'll nod and say, "Not bad."

This subtle manipulation with food has a deep, rich history in my family. When I was younger my mom once tricked me and gave me a veal burger instead of a hamburger. She had read (correctly) that veal is a leaner meat and better for you. So she switched out beef for ground veal (which, I suppose, she cooked herself—which shocks me to think about) and the results were disastrous. "Ugh," I shrieked, toppling over the little yellow plastic table in front of the TV where I ate all my meals. "This burger tastes awful."

My mom never lived that story down. I was outraged that she could be so sneaky. But while I was outraged, I also learned from her. Once she microwaved leftover steak for my dinner and when I refused to eat it she said I better eat it or I'd have to go to bed early and miss *Circus of the Stars*. I was sitting at that same yellow plastic table on a gray shag rug in front of the TV. When she went to the kitchen I took all the steak and shoved it under the rug.

When she came back I told her I had finished and she told me I was a good boy and that I could stay up to watch Bea Arthur juggle tennis balls and behold the spectacle of Brooke Shields walking on broken glass. It was a few days later that the smell revealed my crime. But I'd seen *Circus of the Stars* and I was victorious.

Manipulation is an essential part of the Roberts Family Food Experience. I manipulated my way into cooking dinner by agreeing to cook with my younger brother. My brother and I have a long history of fighting. When I say fighting I don't mean small, petty disagreements. I mean huge, epic battles that rage with the urgency and danger of a classic Greek drama. Over the years, though, we've mellowed out—no more spit fights, pillow warfare, and doors slamming. Now we mostly do our own thing when I come home to visit, which makes cooking together a significant endeavor.

So when the time comes, I fly home for Mother's Day and join Michael and Tali for food shopping at Whole Foods. It is Saturday, the next day is Sunday—Mother's Day, the big dinner—and we are ready to shop.

"Okay," I say to Michael and Tali like a military commander. "We have to begin with produce. We have lots of produce to buy."

In addition to Chicken with 40 Cloves of Garlic, I'm going to make a Greek salad—because I know my family likes Greek salad—then string beans and potatoes for the sides and, for dessert, strawberry shortcake. Since I'm so particular about choosing my fruit and vegetables, I send them off to find sugar.

"What kind of sugar?" asks Michael.

"Just plain ordinary sugar," I say.

"Like in the white bag?" asks Tali.

"Exactly."

They are off, and I begin to choose oranges and lemons for the shortcake (their zests go into the batter). I chose strawberry shortcake for dessert because my dad's mother used to make it for him. Somehow this fact makes the dinner I'm preparing all the more resonant: in a way, this homage to my dad's mother (Elsie, who died before I was born) reveals the power food has to weave the past and present together. Perhaps this cake will awaken in my dad vivid memories from his childhood, while fostering new memories for my brother and me that we can re-create for our children somewhere down the road. The family table is a mystical place where spirits of the past, present, and future collide through smell and taste.

As I consider all this, Tali and Michael return. They are holding a strange-looking plastic jug labeled "organic sugar."

"This is all they have," says Michael.

"Oh," I say. "That's not going to work."

With baking you have to be careful. Though organic sugar *might* work, I don't want to take any chances.

"Put it back," I say, as nicely as I can. "Can you go and see if they have flour?"

"What kind of flour?" asks Tali with a look of concern on her face.

"Just plain, all-purpose flour."

They hurry away and I move on to cucumbers, peppers, and onions. Meanwhile, I've dispatched my mother to Bed Bath & Beyond to buy us a Dutch oven because she has no cooking vessel large enough for six people. Cue my cell phone.

"I'm in Bed Bath and Beyond," she says. "What's it called—the thing you need?"

"A Dutch oven," I tell her.

"A Dutch oven," I hear her repeat to a salesperson there.

A moment of silence as she's led to the Dutch oven section. Buying a Dutch oven might seem a bit lavish for one meal, but my thought is that if I'm cooking for six people—and if I plan to do it again—I'll need a large cooking vessel. And a reasonably priced Dutch oven will serve us well for years to come.

"They have one here. It's Calphalon—is that okay?"

"That's fine."

"I'm going to buy it." A beat and then: "This better be a really good dinner."

Then Michael and Tali return holding a funny-looking bag.

"That's weird organic flour," I chastise. "I'm not sure that'll work the same." (Maybe it will, but I know King Arthur flour will work better.)

"It's all they had," whimpers Tali.

"Well," I conclude. "We'll have to go to Publix."

They look frustrated and they regard me like an alien creature visiting their planet with an agenda they can barely comprehend. This attitude exposes the larger issue, the one that really speaks to what's at play here. I am not the same person I was when I used to live here in Boca Raton—an eager young nerd who thought California Pizza Kitchen and The Cheesecake Factory were the peak of gourmet cuisine. I've gone away—I've gone to college, I've gone to law school, I've gone to writing school. I've been out of Boca for almost ten years and all of my education, all of my life experience, has shaped me into something different, something not entirely similar to what I was. And now I'm attempting to take the food of this new world, this new me, and serve it to my family.

The same question arises from the previous chapter: who am I doing this for—them or me?

The morning of Mother's Day, I am downstairs early. I begin with the cake for the Strawberry Country Cake (a more rustic, countryish spin on traditional shortcake). I'll let the cakes cool while I make everything else. Then when it's time to add the whipped cream and strawberries the cakes will be ready.

Strawberry Country Cake
From *The Barefoot Contessa Parties,* by Ina Garten

Makes two 8-inch cakes. Each cake serves 6 to 8.

$3/4$ cup unsalted butter ($1^1/2$ sticks) at room
   temperature
2 cups sugar
4 extra-large eggs at room temperature
$3/4$ cup sour cream at room temperature
$1/2$ teaspoon grated lemon zest
$1/2$ teaspoon grated orange zest
$1/2$ teaspoon pure vanilla extract
2 cups all-purpose flour
$1/4$ cup cornstarch
$1/2$ teaspoon kosher salt
1 teaspoon baking soda

For the filling for *each* cake:
1 cup heavy whipping cream ($1/2$ pint), chilled
3 tablespoons sugar
$1/2$ teaspoon pure vanilla extract
1 pint fresh strawberries, hulled and sliced

Preheat the oven to 350 degrees. Butter and flour two 8-inch cake pans.

Cream the butter and sugar on high speed until light and fluffy in the bowl of an electric mixer fitted with a paddle attachment. On medium speed, add the eggs, one at a time, then the sour cream, zests, and vanilla, scraping down the bowl as needed. Mix well. In a medium bowl, sift together the flour, corn-starch, salt, and baking soda. On low speed, slowly add the flour mixture to the butter mixture and combine just until smooth.

Pour the batter evenly into the prepared pans, smooth the tops with a spatula, and bake in the center of the oven for 40 to 45 minutes, until a toothpick inserted comes out clean. Let cool in the pans for 30 minutes, then remove to wire racks and let cool to room temperature.

To make the filling for one cake, whip the cream by hand or in a mixer until firm; add the sugar and vanilla. Slice one of the cakes in half with a long, sharp knife. Place the bottom slice of the cake on a serving platter, spread with half of the whipped cream, and scatter with sliced strawberries. Cover with the top slice of the cake and spread with the remaining cream. Decorate with strawberries.

As the cakes are cooling, Michael enters from the gym. "Smells good in here."

"Thanks," I reply. Mom and Dad are in a car headed to Miami. They are going to go shop and eat lunch while Michael and I prepare the dinner.

He goes to take a shower and when he returns I have him chop vegetables for the Greek salad.

Salata Horiatiki, Country (Greek Salad) No. 2
From *The Best Traditional Recipes of Greek Cooking,* by Maria Mavromataki

Makes 5–6 servings

3–4 tomatoes
2 medium-size cucumbers, sliced
1 onion, sliced
5 ounces black olives
2 medium-size green bell peppers, seeded and cut into big pieces
2–3 tablespoons red wine vinegar
3–4 tablespoons olive oil
Salt, oregano
7 ounces feta cheese, cut into chunks

Wash and slice the tomatoes in quarters and place them in a bowl. Add the cucumber, onion, olives, and peppers. Dress the salad with the vinegar, olive oil, salt, and oregano. Add the feta cheese, toss, and serve.

A miracle is taking place on Woodfield Boulevard. Michael finished the salad. Now he's peeling garlic cloves, I'm browning chicken, and we're not fighting.

"Garlic," I say to Michael like a surgeon.

"Garlic," he says, passing the bowl.

I add the forty cloves to the pot and listen to the sizzle. Dinner is on its way.

Chicken with 40 Cloves of Garlic
From *Barefoot in Paris*, by Ina Garten

Serves 6

3 whole heads garlic, about 40 cloves
2 (3 $\frac{1}{2}$-pound) chickens, rinsed and cut into eighths
Kosher salt
Freshly ground black pepper
1 tablespoon unsalted butter
2 tablespoons good olive oil
3 tablespoons Cognac, divided
1 $\frac{1}{2}$ cups dry white wine
1 tablespoon fresh thyme leaves
2 tablespoons all-purpose flour
2 tablespoons heavy cream

Separate the cloves of garlic and drop them into a pot of boiling water for 60 seconds. Drain the garlic and peel. Set aside.

Dry the chicken with paper towels. Season liberally with salt and pepper on both sides. Heat the butter and oil in a large pot or Dutch oven over medium-high heat. In batches, sauté the chicken in fat, skin-side down first, until nicely browned, about

3 to 5 minutes on each side. Turn with tongs or a spatula; you don't want to pierce the skin with a fork. If the fat is burning, turn the heat down to medium. When a batch is done, transfer it to a plate and continue to sauté all the chicken in batches.

Remove the last chicken to the plate and add all of the garlic to the pot. Lower the heat and sauté for 5 to 10 minutes, turning often, until evenly browned. Add 2 tablespoons of the Cognac and all of the wine, return to a boil, and scrape the brown bits from the bottom of the pan. Return the chicken with the juices to the pot and sprinkle with the thyme leaves. Cover and simmer over the lowest heat for about 30 minutes, until all the chicken is done.

Remove the chicken to a platter and cover with aluminum foil to keep warm. In a small bowl, whisk together 1/2 cup of the sauce from the pot and the flour, and then whisk it back into the sauce in the pot. Raise the heat, add the remaining tablespoon of Cognac and the cream, and boil for 3 minutes. Add salt and pepper to taste; it should be very flavorful because chicken tends to be bland. Pour the sauce and the garlic over the chicken and serve hot.

Mom and Dad are back from Miami. The dinner hour soon arrives and so do my grandparents. They come in and admire the smells and the platters of food, as Mom helps me put everything out and find the proper serving utensils and plates. In the final moments of preparation, she sees how capable we are, my brother and I, how self-sufficient. Instead of trying to control us—because she can't, this is not her domain—she simply joins us. Isn't this a good step? Her treating us like adults, not children? Is this the reward for a child cooking his family dinner?

We sit down at the table and everyone looks at the food.

"Dig in," I say, indicating the salad, the platter of chicken, the green beans, and potatoes.

"Mmmm," says Grandma, sampling the garlic sauce. "How many cloves of garlic did you say?"

"Forty."

"Forty," she repeats. "It's delicious."

"It *is* delicious," says Mom.

"Mmm," grunts Dad.

"Very good," says Grandpa.

"I didn't get enough garlic," says Michael.

All seems to be going well—smooth sailing, a happy ending—except for the potatoes. I do a recipe for potatoes that my mom insists will not work. "There's no way those potatoes will get cooked like that in thirty minutes," says my mom.

The process requires Yukon gold potatoes. The potatoes go in a pot with butter, salt, and pepper, the heat is turned on, the lid is placed, and the potatoes are supposed to steam for thirty minutes.

"No way," she says. "Never."

Because my mom doesn't cook, I don't take her seriously. And because I've been away from home, because I've spent the last few years of my life reading about food, I feel a righteous indignation. *Of course these potatoes are going to come out,* I tell myself. *What does she know?*

So when I serve the potatoes, I feel vindicated: the knife goes through a potato and therefore they are cooked.

"Guess you were wrong," I say to my mom teasingly as I serve Grandpa a potato. Grandpa cuts into it, puts it into his mouth, chews for a moment, and spits it out.

"Ad (his nickname for me), it's not cooked." Mom gives me a look. "See?"

I grow sad and she says, "Here, I'll put them in the microwave."

A microwave? At my family dinner? Microwave the potatoes?

But I let Mom take charge at this moment—I let her be a mother—and I sit down and wait for the potatoes to cook.

"Those potatoes were too big," she says. And sure enough, as I later discover, she was right. The recipe (which I should have read more carefully) was for Yukon gold potatoes *two inches* in diameter. These potatoes were much, much bigger.

After a few minutes in the microwave, Mom brings the potatoes back and places them down.

"Now they're cooked," she says.

For every chicken dish and Greek salad we achieve in our adult lives, there arrives an uncooked potato. And sometimes, I realize, we need our mothers to pop those uncooked potatoes into the microwave for us. That is the lesson of the potato.

Cooking dinner for your family, I've discovered, is like therapy. Who would have thought that chopping vegetables could foster such camaraderie between my brother and me? Who knew that garlic sauce would win my grandmother's approval? And who could guess that strawberry shortcake could help establish a richer emotional connection with my dad? (He had two pieces.)

Food is a great equalizer: we all need it to survive, we all have strong feelings about it. For the longest time my family (by way of my mother) felt strongly that a home-cooked meal wasn't worth the effort. And now on this night, because of this book, my family got a taste of what they were missing.

"Everything was delicious," says my mother a few days later, discussing the meal after I've returned to New York.

"Good," I say. "Maybe I'll do it again next time I come home."

There's a pause and then my mom says, "We'll see. It's a lot of work."

It is a lot of work, true, but the greater the work, the greater the reward. "I don't mind," I say. "I like it."

"Okay," she says. "I won't return the Dutch oven, then."

Returning the Dutch oven would have been a clear

acknowledgment that this Mother's Day dinner was a fluke, a strange blip on the static radar of my family's eating habits. Instead, the Dutch oven remains out of the box, in a large kitchen drawer, ready to be used in the future when my family—who now know the joys and comforts of a home-cooked meal—allows me to cook for them again.

EIGHT

Fine Dine like a Professional

Once upon a time I am in South Carolina with my high-school newspaper, *The Galleon*, representing our school at a conference. We meet other students from the Southeast and share our enthusiasm for the fact that Hootie and the Blowfish started their career here at this very spot. We attend writing workshops and panel discussions and then we're taken to the hotel restaurant for dinner. I am sitting with my classmates and a few new people and, after quickly perusing the menu, I tell the waiter that I want the shrimp scampi. The people around me order simpler fare like meat loaf and chicken and spaghetti with meatballs, but I stick to my highly sophisticated shrimp scampi and look forward to its arrival.

And then it arrives and it's covered in sticky, gloppy orange cheese. This is an outrage. The pale, delicate shrimp are being smothered like a geriatric millionaire being suffocated with an orange pillow by a spiteful wife.

"Excuse me," I say to the waiter. "This has cheese on it."

"Yeah?" he says, unsure of my point.

"It didn't say there was cheese on the menu," I murmur.

"We always put cheese on our shrimp scampi."

My classmates and new friends watch curiously, a little bit afraid. I'm only fifteen years old. I'm making a scene.

"I can't eat cheese," I lie. "I can't eat this."

The waiter says he'll bring the manager.

He goes off and my new friends quickly say to me, "Just eat it. Take the cheese off."

"No. It didn't say there was cheese on the menu."

The manager comes over and says, "What's the problem here?"

I tell him the situation and he says, "Shrimp scampi always has cheese. It's how it's made."

I know this isn't true because I've had shrimp scampi at various other restaurants and if it has any cheese at all (which it seldom does) it's Parmesan, not *orange* cheese.

"Well, I can't eat cheese: I'm allergic."

That's a lie and the manager eyes me dubiously. "So scrape it off."

One of the teachers with us on the trip comes over to see what the trouble is. When she learns the situation she apologizes to the manager and tells me just to eat it. All my new friends and cohorts look extremely embarrassed. I stare down at my plate, scrape off the cheese, and carve at the shrimp. For seventeen dollars there are only two meager shrimp and they're overcooked. But I eat my shrimp and shut my mouth and wonder what I've done wrong, why everyone around me is so embarrassed, and how I should've handled the situation. It would take twelve years and a date with a food-writing legend to learn the answers.

When Moses received the Ten Commandments he had to work for them: he had to climb Mount Sinai without so much as a grappling hook to receive the written word of God. Similarly, it takes unimaginable concentration and effort to track down and engage the food world's supreme dining deity, Ruth Reichl, former restaurant critic for the *New York Times* and current editor-in-chief of *Gourmet* magazine. For this, my chapter on dining out, I need someone who knows the ropes, who can guide me and my readers out of the desert and onto a path toward better dining, to truly understand how to experience a restaurant. But unlike God, Ruth Reichl hasn't summoned me with a burning bush. I have to summon her with an e-mail and the help of several friends. I don't expect her to write back but she does. We make a date for lunch on July 19 at 1 p.m. at Esca.

When the time comes, I am a nervous wreck. I am standing outside the restaurant at 12:30 pacing back and forth like a death row inmate thirty minutes before execution. I am a perpetually early person and here my earliness does not serve me well. I factored this in, actually, when leaving my apartment. "Don't leave too early," I told myself. "Or you'll get there too early and you'll be a nervous wreck."

But there I am outside, pacing. It's a beautiful day out—the sun is shining but it's not too hot. Esca has an outdoor section that several diners are enjoying as I gaze upon them. I try to inform them, with my superb nonverbal communication skills, that the person I'm about to eat with is far more important than the person they're eating with. "Ruth Reichl," my eyeballs whisper. "Eat that!"

And then there she is.

I'm standing in front of the menu again—I've read it fifty or sixty times—and in my peripheral vision I see her on the corner, quickly approaching where I'm standing. She is wearing a black jacket and black pants, and her black bangs hang iconically over her eyes.

I immediately swivel away: I don't want to seem too eager. But then I quickly swivel back: I don't want to seem too unfriendly. And before I know it I'm upon her.

"Hi, Ruth," I say, putting out my hand.

"Hi, you're Adam," she says, reaching out and shaking my hand.

"Yes. It's so nice to meet you. Thank you so much for doing this."

She nods and I hold the door for her as we enter the restaurant. The staff descends.

It's fascinating to see how everyone reacts to her. They try to keep their cool, but there's a nervous energy in the air. The small talk isn't really small talk. It's "let's pretend we're not awed by your presence" talk. Yet, there's also a sense of familiarity: this isn't the first time Ruth's been here. In fact, that's one of the first things she tells me when we sit down at a corner table—a perfect table—perhaps the nicest table in the restaurant. It is here that her first proclamation is made.

The First Commandment: Be a Regular

"The first thing I can tell you about eating out," she says in her sage, unpretentious voice, "is that it pays to be a regular. You should tell your readers to pick a few restaurants and to go often."

She is sitting in the seat that faces the restaurant. I'm next to her—not across from her, but next to her—and I'm facing out the window, into the courtyard.

"It's a treat to be treated like family," she continues. "You've earned that right when you're a regular."

This idea makes sense intuitively. Eating, as we learned in the dating chapter, is an intimate act. Going out to eat, then, is an exercise in intimacy: it's a private act that happens in the public sphere. A restaurant cooks food that you put into your body. You want to go to a place that you can trust but that, despite the familiarity, can still surprise you on a regular basis. And once a restaurant has won you over it's natural that you'd want to return again and again to allow the relationship to develop the way you would with a friend or a paramour. What Ruth is advocating is restaurant monogamy: all the perks of being exclusive in a human relationship apply with a restaurant.

Consider my parents. They are more than regulars at their favorite restaurant in Boca Raton, a steak house called New York Prime. They eat there weekly—it's my father's Platonic ideal of a restaurant—and because they go so often, they have their favorite table reserved for them each week (they don't need to make a reservation, they only call to *cancel* that week's table). Their favorite waiter, Mo, brings olives and orange slices from the bar for them to snack on before the meal starts; he knows my dad's drink (Tanqueray and tonic), he knows how my mother and father each like their salads (my father without cheese, my mother with dressing on the side), and he takes the time to distribute the side dishes for them instead of plopping the platters of onion rings and creamed spinach onto the table. My parents buy Christmas gifts for the manager, the hostess, and Mo, and they are rewarded on birthdays when the staff treats our family to magnificent portions of chocolate cake, adorned with whipped cream and happy birthday greetings written in icing.

Another example is the place where I've written most of this book: Joe: The Art of Coffee. I am such a regular there that when I don't order my usual drink (an iced latte in summer, a cappuccino in winter) it throws the staff off. The owner, Jonathan Rubinstein, knows me and what I do for a living. "How's the book?" he asks as I sit with my laptop, typing away. "Good," I say, and then I ask how his other stores are doing. The next time I come he gives me my drink for free. "This one's on me," he says, and I am rewarded for being a regular.

"Exactly," says Ruth, who listens to these stories with kind interest. "It really pays to be a regular."

A waiter approaches and asks if we'd like anything to drink.

"Water's fine," says Ruth.

I nod my approval. She seems to be studying me, trying to make me out: *Who is this strange person I'm eating lunch with? What's his deal?*

Then a large man in chef's whites approaches us. This, I quickly discern (I'm very discerning), is the chef, David Pasternack.

"How's it going?" he asks in his gruff but charming manner. I'm a bit starstruck: David is one of New York's most distinguished chefs, the winner of numerous awards and accolades, and the subject of a memorable *New Yorker* article by Mark Singer that came out a few years earlier. The article detailed David's dual life as chef and fisherman: he catches much of the fish they serve at Esca.

"David," Ruth says. "This is Adam. He's The Amateur Gourmet."

David gives her a quizzical look and then looks at me. "The Amateur Gourmet, huh," he says. He shakes my hand. "You're going to have to give up the title once you're not an amateur anymore."

Ruth asks after his daughter, he asks after her family. They talk about the weather—it's been painfully hot for the past several weeks.

Then Ruth does something that she'll advocate later, her second commandment of dining out.

The Second Commandment: Ask for Help

Ruth asks David: "Is there anything special on the menu today?"

"The corn salad," he answers.

"Really?" asks Ruth. "Is it really time for corn?" (It's mid-July.)

"We found some sweet corn," he says. "It's surprisingly good for this time of year."

She nods. "Anything else?"

"We've got a king crab," he says. "Straight from Alaska." Ruth nods again.

"Okay. Enjoy." He exits to the kitchen.

"That's something most people don't do when they go out to eat," explains Ruth. "It's a myth that if you ask questions they'll give you what the chef wants to get rid of. That's simply not true."

Granted, she's Ruth Reichl and of course they want her to have the best they have to offer. But it makes sense that at a restaurant like Esca, where the food varies day to day by the quality of the fish—what's a fresh catch and what isn't—that you should ask what's worth ordering. The more you ask the more informed you are as a consumer. That's true in other contexts: when you buy a house or rent an apartment, you ask lots of questions. You ask questions before a doctor does a procedure, you ask questions when a travel agent books your trip. Why shouldn't you ask questions when you're out to eat? As with all those other contexts, eating out is an investment: you're investing in the quality of your meal. Why not ensure that you're getting the most for your money?

Ruth agrees and reiterates the point with wine. "It's the same with the sommelier," she says. "They're happy to help you also—that's what they're paid for."

I had an illuminating experience last year with the food blogger Derrick Schneider (of "An Obsession with Food" —www.obsessionwithfood.com) and his wife, Melissa. We went to Craft for dinner and Derrick, a wine maven, studied the wine list with intense concentration. Instead of ordering wine, however, he first saw what we were going to order for dinner. Once we decided—most of us chose red meat—he spoke to the sommelier about a proper red wine. The sommelier offered knowing suggestions about which wines would complement which dishes, and steered us toward his personal favorites. It's wonderful to engage a passionate person in the thing he or she is passionate about, and that's particularly true of sommeliers.

Of course my parents were suspicious of this when we went to dinner a few weeks later. "They'll try to sell you the most expensive bottle," my mom insisted.

"But," I said, "you can ask for help choosing an *inexpensive* wine."

"Then why don't you do it?"

So I put my money where my mouth was and asked the sommelier for help choosing an inexpensive white to go with the tasting menu we'd ordered.

"Of course," he said and then helped us choose a reasonable Riesling that won raves from everyone at the table.

"See?" I said to my parents as they sipped and nodded their approval. All of this because of asking questions, asking for help.

And if Ruth Reichl can ask for help, so can you.

When the menus arrive, we both begin to study. Ordering lunch with Ruth Reichl is a nerve-wracking experience. What she orders is presumably the *right* thing to order—after all, she's this chapter's professional—but it's tacky and unimpressive to copy her.

"I think I'll start with the king crab he recommended," she says.

"Hmmm," I say. "Maybe I should have that too."

There's a pause and then I backpedal. "Unless you want me to order something different. Is that the right thing to do?"

"What do you want to do?"

This leads us directly to the third commandment.

The Third Commandment: Know Your Hunger

Reader, I'm sure you've gone for a nice meal and struggled over what to order. Do you order what the restaurant's known for? Do you order the dish you read about in the *New York Times*? Do you order what your friend orders? Do you order something different?

"I mean," I continue, "isn't it bad to order what the other person orders? Isn't it better to try a few things?"

"Back when I was a critic I used to make everyone order something different," she says. "So I kind of like it when someone orders the same thing. It reminds me that I'm not a critic anymore."

I consider this and then I see the crudo (raw marinated fish) listed under the antipasto. "Oh," I say gleefully. "My friend Pim said I should order the crudo and champagne— that it would impress you."

"Do you want champagne?"

"No. Not really."

"I can't drink at lunch," she says. "I'll be done for."

Of course, Ruth is intimately familiar with her body and how it reacts to food and wine. This is the state of awareness required for effective dining: you have to know what you're hungry for, what you need and don't need to enjoy your meal.

"Plus you have to go back to work," I say. "You don't want to show up drunk, you'll get fired!"

She smiles kindly at my joke and then we discuss entrées.

"Why is there a box around the salmon?" I ask.

"The box calls attention to the fact that salmon season is almost over," she explains. "Wild Alaskan salmon is really special," she adds. "Have you ever had wild Alaskan salmon?"

"I don't think so."

"Hmmm," she says, reading. "I think I'm going to start with the crab and then have the linguine with clams."

Ordering is an art, you see. Her choices complement each other: the crab will provide rich buttery protein and the linguine will satisfy a craving for carbs.

"I think I'll try the salmon," I say cheerfully. "The crudo and the salmon. Or is that too much fish?"

"Well, do you like fish?" she asks.

"Yes," I say.

"Then it's not too much fish."

Ruth is clearly coaxing me out of my world of worry into a place of self-knowledge. *What do you want?* she's asking. *What are you hungry for?*

What she knows and what I'm learning is that dining out is about satisfying hunger. Ordering something you're not hungry for is a recipe for dissatisfaction. I search within and decide that I *am* hungry for crudo—my curiosity, at least, is hungry—and I am hungry for salmon. I tell the waiter when he comes and he says, "Very good, sir."

Very good. I'm doing okay.

At this point, there's light conversation about her family and her son ("Is he more like you or his father?" I ask. "Oh, he's just like me," she says and then describes his seventeenth birthday, which involved his eating across the boroughs). She asks where I'm from and when I say Florida she says, "You weren't born there, were you?" She's sussed me out: my New York Jewish inflections give everything away. (Three words always reveal my roots: *Fla*rida, *arr*ange, and *harr*ible.)

We discuss farmer's markets (I tell her that Amanda Hesser coached me through my second chapter) and I bring up the fact that farmer's markets can be prohibitively expensive. She responds, "Food isn't cheap. People used to spend half their income on food. Now they spend 6 percent. That's a huge difference."

Then, somehow, the conversation arrives at a place that I will regret later. I tell her how nervous I was to meet her, that I was worried all week, and that (gulp, I so regret it now) I spent an hour before lunch deciding whether to wear pants or jeans.

Her response is direct. It provides our fourth commandment.

The Fourth Commandment: Wear What You Want

"Why?" she asks straightforwardly.

Why. Why. Well: getting dressed up has always been a big part of going out to eat for my family and me. My parents and people of their generation put so much weight on appearance and what's appropriate that it's snaked its way into my consciousness. "Definitely pants," said my mom when I asked her advice. Of course she said pants: my parents are pants people.

But Pim disagreed. "Jeans," she told me. "You don't want to look like you're trying too hard."

The impression I get from Ruth Reichl is that, like choosing what to order, choosing what to wear should only be a function of you and your own desires. Wear what you want to wear. And if a restaurant isn't hospitable to what you want to wear, don't eat there. It's about you, she seems to be saying. It's about you and what you want. I infer all of this from her one-word answer, "Why?"

Our appetizers arrive. My crudo is presented quite beautifully on a glass plate with three segments, two of which look like normal slivers of raw fish and one that is much darker and topped with a dark cherry.

"What kind of fish is that?" Ruth asks the waiter.

"Spearfish," he says. Then he corrects himself: "Actually," he says, "the one in the middle is spearfish."

When he leaves, Ruth asks me if she can try a bite.

"Sure," I say.

The Fifth Commandment: Share Your Food

Amanda Hesser writes in *Cooking for Mr. Latte* that she hates sharing her food at restaurants. "When I go out to a restaurant, I do not like feeling as if I'm at a buffet. I like to construct my meal thoughtfully and then eat it. I don't want to pass plates and I don't want someone plopping a slab of his skate in my lamb jus."

But Ruth Reichl clearly disagrees. She stabs her fork into my fish and cuts a piece for herself. She tastes it and makes a face. She says, "It looks funny and it *tastes* funny."

Now Ruth's experience of Esca is enhanced: she's sampled more food than she would have if she only ate her own. And speaking of her own, her king crab leg, which lays across the plate in front of her, is glorious. The meat is oozing with butter and Ruth looks at it and smiles radiantly. (She has the most radiant smile I've ever seen: she could play the sun in a school play.)

"Here," she says. "You have to have a bite. There's nothing like king crab."

I don't refuse her offer and I stab my fork in. I bring a piece to my lips and taste. It's heavenly: warm, sweet, and unctuous. "Wow," I say and I can see that Ruth is glad.

Sharing, I discover, is more than just broadening your experience of a restaurant's food. Sharing makes the experience more communal; it unites a table in the experience of pleasure. Sharing food is like sharing your toys: the thrill is doubled when there's an audience. Knowing that Ruth has sampled my crudo I eat it with more intelligence; knowing that I've sampled her crab, she eats it, perhaps, with more pride.

"These things cost two hundred dollars each," she explains. "They ship them here live."

"It's a dangerous industry, isn't it?" I ask. "There's a TV show about it."

But Ruth is focused on her crab, so I return to my crudo. The raw fish is slippery but elegantly dressed. I like the cherry with the one that she said was funny-tasting, but I don't like it as much as I like her crab. Which is the one unfortunate consequence of sharing: jealousy. I want more king crab and I can't have any more. The sharing period is now over.

The antipasto plates are swept away and the entrées arrive.

"That crab was so filling," says Ruth as they place the linguine with briny mahogany clams, red pepper, and pancetta before her. "I don't think I can eat all this."

A waiter sets down my dish—Salmone Selvatico: Yukon River Wild King Salmon with Black Mission Figs, Watercress, and Saba Vinaigrette.

It's a beautiful thing and Ruth admires it.

"That salmon looks perfect," she says.

"Taste it," I say and she doesn't refuse.

"Mmmm," she says. "I don't normally love salmon but that's excellent."

Ruth offers some of her pasta and I taste—a difficult thing to do without making a mess ("Make sure to get a clam," she advises)—and I stab a clam, taste, and nod my approval.

"That's great," I say. She sighs and eats a few strands more. "That crab was very filling."

Then a waiter comes with a bowl of the corn salad. "A gift from the chef," he says.

Ruth studies the salad carefully.

The Sixth Commandment: Be Intelligently Critical

The waiter exits and Ruth tastes. The salad immediately fails her scrutiny.

"This isn't good," she says matter-of-factly. "The corn isn't good—it's starchy, it doesn't have much flavor."

I taste too and nod my agreement.

"Whatever flavor it has," she continues, "is obscured by the goat cheese, the chanterelles, and the nuts."

This prognosis is thoughtfully delivered and done so in a way that justifies her status as a great arbiter of taste. She's articulate in a way that most diners aren't because they don't know how to be. Her pronouncements are those of a good writer: they are specific. She doesn't say "yummy" or "bad." She says "the corn is starchy" and "the flavor is obscured." She knows her field, she knows how to analyze, she knows how to be critical.

And this is true of anyone who's passionate about a subject. Ask a movie buff what he thinks of the new Almodovar film and he'll answer you with great enthusiasm and flair. Ask a wrestling fan how he feels about cage matches, and he'll wax lyrical for hours. The lesson is that once you care about food, once you care about dining, you will pay more attention. Understand why some dishes succeed while others fail, notice how a dish is composed, what flavors it contains, how those flavors are contrasted, the freshness of the ingredients, the level of seasoning, the overall balance. Once you start noticing these things your ability to judge a restaurant on its merits will improve immeasurably. Ruth Reichl got to where she is because she paid attention. She pays attention now and I attempt to do the same.

"I agree with what you're saying," I say, "but I like the chanterelles. They're well prepared."

She shakes her head and pushes the bowl away. When the waiter clears it I notice him notice that it remains uneaten.

Much of Ruth's linguine remains uneaten as well. This leads us to another commandment:

The Seventh Commandment: Eat Until You're Full

It's a simple fact that many meals are ruined by overeating.

"I can't believe I ate so much," is a common refrain. Or: "My stomach's going to explode." Or: "You don't understand me, you'll never understand me, I'm a complicated person. And I ate too much bread!"

The lesson Ruth Reichl silently offers is to stop when you're full. Don't overdo it. Unless you have an endless appetite and, like me, you can clean everything off your plate and still have room for dessert. Otherwise, be like Ruth and stop when you're full.

● ● ●

We are at the end of the meal. How have I performed? Should I have eaten less of my food? More of hers? Should I have ordered champagne just to show my confidence, my ability to exert myself?

"I hope this was helpful," she says. "Will this be good for your book?"

"Yes," I say eagerly. "I wonder if I could ask you a few more questions."

"Sure," she says as I take out my pad.

"This is being written for people who don't know much about dining out," I say. "I just want to make sure we cover everything—"

"Mmmhmmm," says Ruth.

"So to start, what should someone know about a restaurant before they get there? Like if someone were coming here, should they just come without knowing anything first?"

The Eighth Commandment: Know Where You're Eating

"Well," she says, "they might want to know it's an Italian restaurant. And they might want to know that the restaurant specializes in fish."

I write this down and nod my head. Yes, yes, of course. In the age of the Internet, one doesn't really have an excuse not to know where he is eating. Simply typing the name of a restaurant into Google will yield more information than you can fathom. Type "Esca" into Google and you can be an expert in no time.

"Cool," I say. "And when you get here, with a menu like this, how much should the average person order? One from each column?"

The Ninth Commandment: Don't Order One from Each Column Unless You Want To

"Oh, God, no," says Ruth. "No one eats that much at lunch. Unless you *want* to—if you're hungry for it."

Yes, yes, I think as I write. *Yes, this makes sense—too much food for lunch.*

"And how should you choose what to order?"

The Tenth Commandment: I Am Not the Lord Your God, There Are No Commandments

Ruth, who's been patient this whole meal, suddenly bursts like a balloon.

"Adam," she says abruptly. "Stop it with the word *should*!"

I drop my pen.

"There is no should when it comes to dining out! This isn't about right or wrong, this isn't a test. This is about *pleasure.*"

She gets louder as she speaks. "Just because I like something or do something doesn't mean it's the right thing to eat or do. It's a matter of opinion. Everyone's afraid of doing something wrong when they eat—"

I gulp.

"—but there *is* no right or wrong. This is a *service industry*. Nobody," she says pointedly, "*nobody* should be intimidated in a restaurant, ever."

My heart is beating fast.

"People need to be bolder about this stuff," she says with exasperation. "People should get what they *want*."

She tells me about her husband, Michael, whom she calls the reluctant gourmet. "Michael is the worst pain in the ass," she says. "He's married to someone who can have the world literally at his feet and he doesn't want it. If there's a tasting menu he says 'I don't want a tasting menu . . . I just want *this, this, and this*. That's what I *want*.'"

Immediately I am whisked back to South Carolina where my fifteen-year-old self is outraged over shrimp smothered in orange cheese. Though I'm too young to be so vocal, and though I'm being disrespectful and bratty and making a scene, my indignation matches Ruth Reichl's: this is *my* money and I should get what I want.

Rules of propriety and etiquette are stifling—they're archaic—and they prevent people from truly enjoying the pleasures that restaurants have to offer. That's what Ruth is here to teach me: how to get the most pleasure out of eating out. She doesn't worry over rules—there are no commandments, only suggestions—and she wants to empower me to understand my desires and to feed them. She's a rebel—she was a rebel at the *Times* when she gave three-star reviews to ethnic restaurants (totally taboo at the time), and she's a rebel today. She charges forth and does as she wants and the world bows before her, not the other way around.

This is a woman who knows her own desires. When the waiter asks if we want dessert she says no, unless I want some. I do want some but I don't need it here—I can get some later.

Then, when the waiter lays down forks and knives and plates it's clear there's a dessert coming. And sure enough, another waiter emerges with a dark chocolate cake glistening with ice cream on a plate.

"Compliments of the house," he says.

"I'm going to *kill* you," Ruth responds.

"I'm not going to touch that," she says to me when he exits. "You can have some if you want."

And knowing what I want—the gift Ruth Reichl has given me—I lift my fork and dig in.

"Thanks," I say as I shovel chocolate cake into my mouth. Maybe it's rude to eat cake when the other person isn't eating. Maybe it's wrong to eat it so fast—she's ready to go, starting to rise from the table—but ignoring the rules is the lesson I've learned today. She's empowered me, empowered me to have my cake and eat it too. The smooth chocolate coats my tongue and the back of my throat and I feel a warmth all over, the warmth that comes from forgetting commandments and the word *should* and answering your body's call for what it really wants.

NINE

Dine Alone

L'Atelier de Joël Robuchon is the much lauded experimental restaurant vision of superstar French chef Joël Robuchon. His is a name that Parisians speak of with great reverence: there's no disputing the fact that Joël Robuchon is a living legend.

It is December and I have journeyed to Paris with my friend John. We have planned our trip based on how much time each of us has available to us: I have a whole week, John only has a few days. So we spend four days together and then John leaves. I am alone.

When we are together, John and I (and his brother Chris, who visits from Geneva) nosh at homey Paris eateries: bistros, like Chez Omar, where the steak frites we consume have John licking his plate. "If I were going to be executed," he says, "this would be my last meal."

John and Chris prefer to stay on budget and I know that if I am going to visit L'Atelier Joël Robuchon—where a meal promises to be well over a hundred euros (around $130)—I will have to go alone.

Dining by myself, though, is a scary prospect. It's not a coincidence, perhaps, that "dining alone" sounds so much like "dying alone." For many, the fear of dining alone is the same fear that causes them to marry the wrong person, to maintain destructive friendships, and to participate in group suicide. Dining alone is an open display of solitude, loneliness made visible, and it's a statement to the world that despite all your better qualities there isn't a person on this earth who wants to sit opposite you watching you chew.

My friend Alex told me once that when she was younger she used to cry when she saw people eating by themselves. "I felt so bad for them. I thought it was the saddest thing in the world."

My mother sometimes, to earn my pity, will describe an afternoon of eating by herself. "I miss you," she'll say. "I wish you were here. I ate all alone today in my car, outside the bagel store."

The image of my mother in her car, pressed up against the steering wheel eating a bagel out of a paper bag is, indeed, pitiable. Why is that? Why do people dining alone arouse such wellsprings of empathy in us? Aren't they just nourishing themselves? Do we pity someone drinking water from a water fountain? Do we shed a tear for the guy eating trail mix in the park?

The key word, I believe, is *dining*. There is a difference between grabbing a sandwich at a local deli and sitting down to a Michelin-starred meal by yourself. One is an act of necessity, the other an act of luxury. Society understands when lone individuals who are hungry sit down to grab a bite for lunch. It is less forgiving when that same individual puts on a suit, combs his hair, sprays on cologne, and journeys to a restaurant by himself and asks for a table for one. Yet, this is exactly what I plan to do on this night, the night that I set out to dine at L'Atelier Joël Robuchon by myself.

I did my research earlier in the day: according to my *Time Out Guide to Paris,* L'Atelier Joël Robuchon does not accept reservations. The setup is a large counter where people sit and watch the chefs prepare their food. I find this thought comforting: I won't be alone at a table, I will be at a counter like Norm on *Cheers.* Is Norm self-conscious when he orders his beer? Of course not. Why should I be self-conscious when I order my foie gras? I'm going to be fine.

I have dined by myself many times in America, but nowhere this fancy. I will sit for quick panini at 'ino, a lobster roll at Pearl Oyster Bar, or a Greek salad at Snack Taverna without too much self-consciousness. Almost always it's for lunch and almost always I bring a magazine. Most often it's the *New Yorker:* a perfect quick-meal companion. I can skim the cartoons, read the "Talk of the Town," read the reviews. If there's a long article that catches my eye, I can start it when I place my order and finish it on the subway home. The *New Yorker* makes me feel safe and not alone. The question arises, as I finish getting dressed, can I bring the *New Yorker* in my bag—the winter fiction issue—to L'Atelier Joël Robuchon? Or will that be cheating? Will I really be there if I am safe in my comfort zone? Plus, will that look funny to arrive at the restaurant in my puffy winter jacket with a magazine under my arm?

I decide to leave it behind. I venture forth alone and determined. I am going to dine at one of Paris's most revered restaurants, I tell myself. This will be an experience I will never forget.

The journey from the hotel to the restaurant is quite involved. John and I found our hotel online—we booked a discount trip on virginvacations.com. We got our airfare and hotel for the astonishing price of $449. As the adage goes, we got what we paid for: our hotel is dingy and far away from everything in the seventeeth "far away from everything" arrondissement. For the first few nights there, we have no hot water. Maybe the hotel's dinginess is part of its charm, but at this moment—dressed, coiffed, and cologned—I wish I were at a palatial hotel with tuxedoed employees escorting me to the Rolls Royce waiting for me outside. "Merci," I would say, slipping wads of euros into their grateful palms. As it stands, I give my room key to the man at the front desk, who regards me coolly.

"You still have electric converter?" he asks.

This is a bone of contention between us. I forgot to purchase power converters in America and thus can't plug in any of my electronics. I asked at the front desk for one earlier in the week and this man said, "Okay, for one hour, yes."

"One hour? I need for longer than that!"

"Okay," he said with arched eyebrow. "You bring back when finished."

Since then, every time I return my room key to the desk—a required procedure before leaving the hotel—he asks for the converter. I exploit the language barrier and play dumb.

"Yes, yes," I say. "I have it. Thank you." I exit with a flourish and proceed on the twenty-minute walk to the nearest Métro stop: Malesherbes.

I love that word, Malesherbes. The reason I love it is that I purposely mispronounce it in my head. The right way to say it, in French, is Mailz*airb*. I pronounce it male-sherb-eez. Like herpes.

I ride the Métro to the rue du Bac stop and exit a bit nervously.

Here I am: 8 p.m. on a Wednesday night in Paris, about to dine alone at a highly distinguished, highly expensive restaurant. Who do I think I am? Most Americans my age are eating at the Olive Garden right now; why do I deserve any better? More important: how will I look to them, these fancified French people sipping aged wine in designer clothes speaking a language I barely comprehend? Not only do I not comprehend it, I mock it. Male-sherb-eez, anyone?

Maybe I should turn around, I think loudly, the voice in

my head getting more and more panicky. I could go to a low-key bistro and eat steak frites like I did with John and his brother. But here I am in a suit—a suit masked by a puffy North Face jacket—and cologned and coiffed; I can't turn back now.

I continue, following the directions in my hand. When I get close, the area grows increasingly more refined: fancy hotels, fancy stores, fancy people leaving fancy hotels to shop at fancy stores. And there it is: festooned in red Christmas lights, L'Atelier Joël Robuchon, looking exclusive and imposing yet ever so slightly welcoming.

Peering through the windows, I see what I expect to see: a large counter space with well-dressed Parisians eating and sipping wine while facing a kitchen. This isn't so scary after all. I can handle this. I will fit right in.

I approach the door. Here's the plan: I will open it, greet the host—"Bon soirée," I will say—and then declare my intention: "One." "Un," in French. "Table for un."

The door has no handle, so I push. When doors have no handles you push. Yet, I am surprised to find that when I push nothing happens.

"That's odd," says the nervous voice in my head.

I push again. Still nothing.

Then I do something I never expected to do: I dig my fingers into the wood paneling and try to pull it open. This plan works poorly. The door doesn't budge.

"What kind of restaurant is this?" I think, the voice in my head enraged. "The door doesn't open!"

Just then, the door opens. An older Frenchman dressed elegantly stands there with a clipboard.

"Bon soirée," he says, eyeing me, perhaps suspiciously. "How can I help you?" he asks in French.

"Ah, yes," I stammer. "Bon soirée . . . table por un."

He stares at me, confused.

"Pardon?"

"Parlez-vous anglais?" I squeak.

"Oui," he says.

"Table for one?"

He stares again. I feel him take in my puffy jacket. "But there's a suit underneath!" I want to tell him.

"I'm sorry," he says. "Is impossible."

"Oh," I say.

"We are completely booked, monsieur." He shows me his clipboard filled with names.

I stand out there in the cold night air and feel myself deflate. All this planning, all this dressing, all these nerves frayed for nothing.

"Isn't there anything?" I plead.

"No, I'm afraid," he says, shaking his head. "Only eleven-thirty," he says, as if eleven-thirty would be the most absurd time for anyone to eat in the history of eating.

Eleven-thirty. It is eight-thirty now: that would be three hours. I could wait three hours, couldn't I? Besides, this man might be bluffing. What if I call his bluff?

"Eleven-thirty," I repeat. "Okay," I say. "Eleven-thirty."

He gives me a look that says: "You can't be serious."

I return with a look that insists: "I am serious."

"Okay, monsieur, what is your name?"

"Adam," I stammer. Of course, I should have said my last name but Adam is what comes out.

"Very good, monsieur Adam, eleven-thirty," he concludes, closing the door behind him. I breathe in deeply: I've done it! I've penetrated the inner sanctum of finer French cuisine! Now I need to kill three hours in a strange part of town in a country where I don't speak the language.

Next door is a beautiful hotel, the sort that matches the fantasy hotel I had in my head when I was leaving my ramshackle hotel in the seventeenth. I see beautiful people dressed beautifully traipsing through the marbled lobby and then exiting in their fur coats into polished cars. Could I sit in this hotel lobby and kill three hours?

I know the answer is no—they'd surely ask me to leave—and then I wonder why. Why don't I feel entitled to go sit in that lobby? Well, okay, I'm not a guest there: I'm not entitled. But something more is at play. The self-doubt that forbids me from entering that lobby is the same self-doubt that plagued me on my way to the restaurant. Once again: who do I think I am? What gives me the right to enjoy the splendors reserved for people twice my age who have accomplished great things in their lives?

What have I accomplished? I was voted "Most Likely to Be Famous" my senior year of high school. I won the Palm Beach County fair-housing songwriting contest for a song called "My Eyes Just See Gray." My mom came up with the title.

Who am I to walk among titans: to share their couches, to eat their food? I know this sentiment is shared by most of my friends. Lisa, for example, uses the word *fancy* to describe the restaurants I enjoy in America. "Okay, I'll go eat your fancy food with you," she'll say when I talk her into going somewhere slightly more expensive than, say, the Olive Garden.

People our age belong at the Olive Garden. All-you-can-eat bread, all-you-can-eat salad: this is value, this is what young people enjoy. Why do we deserve any better?

Maybe we don't think we deserve better because we don't have access to anything better. Money, prestige: these are the things that allow one access to the finer things in life, aren't they? Restaurants often succeed and fail based on the buzz surrounding them. It's the Studio 54 effect: the proverbial velvet rope is what makes entry desirable. If everyone were granted entry, it wouldn't be that special to enter, would it? The door to L'Atelier Joël Robuchon is the perfect metaphor: it only opens from the inside.

It only opens from the inside, that is, unless you stand out there and you persist. Ultimately it has to open: people have to leave, other people need to enter. You can fall prey to the smoke and mirrors that convince you not to enter or you can enter. The only question that remains is, will it be worth the effort?

As I ponder all this, I make my way past the hotel to a bookstore. Here's a democratic institution if there ever was one. The finest books sit alongside the pulpiest trash and it's left to the shopper to sort through them. You can spend

$6.99 on Jackie Collins or Dostoyevsky, it's your decision. Here, though, all the books are in French. All the books, that is, except the books on one shelf labeled "Anglais."

I spend the next three hours thumbing through the "Anglais" shelf and then the time comes to return to the restaurant. I purchase a book by Zadie Smith—*On Beauty*—that I fall for in that three-hour period. I tuck it into my coat pocket as a security blanket: maybe I will need some reading material after all. I'm feeling pretty vulnerable.

I make my way back to the restaurant and stand outside in the cold and wait for the door to open. This is terrifying and humiliating: standing outside a door that only opens from the inside, you feel completely judged by the world. And when it doesn't open for a few minutes you feel your-self judged poorly. Who are they to judge me poorly? Maybe I should judge them poorly and just go eat some oysters and call it a night.

Finally, it opens and two severely well-dressed couples exit laughing. I expect them to hand me their valet tickets but instead the host emerges behind them and, recognizing me, says: "Ah, Monsieur Adam, right this way."

My heart beats fast. I follow him into the restaurant, take off my jacket, and soak in the scenery as he leads me to a tall chair between two couples at the long communal bar overlooking the kitchen. He asks for my jacket and I quickly remove the Zadie Smith book from the coat pocket, just in case I need it. I also remove a Moleskine notebook, a pen, and a camera.

"You have all you need, sir?" quips the host.

"Oui," I say. "Merci."

I sit down and take in my surroundings. Ah, here I am. I have arrived. The room is dark. I have no menu. I smile at a waitress pouring wine for an older gentleman who scrutinizes her with his eyes. She doesn't smile back.

I place the Zadie Smith book, the Moleskine notebook, the camera, and the pen on the counter in front of me. The man to my right shoots me a glance and then looks back at his wife. I wait a few moments to be acknowledged by the waitress. As I wait, I lift the Moleskine and the pen and begin to write:

12/21/05
L'Atelier de Joël Robuchon
Thoughts as gathered at dinner at the bar.
Red menus, red glasses . . .
Everything is a bit of a battle here . . . for the table,
for the waitress's attention.

Just then the waitress comes over.

"Bon soirée," she says. Then she says something else in French and I say, as I've grown accustomed to saying, "Parlez vous anglais?"

"Oui," she answers.

She hands me a menu and asks me what I would like to drink. I tell her I am going to have the tasting menu—which, I believe, surprises her a bit. This is a serious thing to order for someone so young and American sitting awkwardly at the bar with a book, a notebook, a pen, and a camera in front of him.

"What wine do you recommend for the tasting menu?" I query.

She removes a wine list from a shelf. She points to the wine by the glass and suggests the Pinot Blanc. The price isn't too outrageous so I give the nod. She scurries off.

Now I feel very alone. The couples to my left and right are really chatting it up. I lift the Zadie Smith book and try to read from where I left off in the store but it's too dark. I return it to the counter and stare into the kitchen. I see a chef carving long pieces of meat off a leg with a hoof on it.

The hoof is a powerful image and I stare at it, captivated. This hoof, this animal foot that once traipsed across prairies and through mountain springs, reminds me that I am a meat-eater, a carnivore who stands fiercely atop the food chain. Why am I nervous to be here? I am a mighty, powerful, bloodthirsty beast. I'm a brave warrior surrounded by fellow warriors. That's what I'm missing, I realize: a sense of entitlement. By biological imperative, I am entitled to be here. That's not *my* leg the chef is carving with a long, sharp blade.

The waitress returns with my wine and I thank her with a beastlike "merci." Then she places a bread basket on the counter in front of me and exits.

I take a piece of bread, spread it with butter, and take a bite. I wash it down with wine and nod my approval.

Then something peculiar happens. The man to my right puts his hand on my bread basket and slides it so it's in front of him and his female companion. He doesn't take any bread out of it, he just slides it possessively and returns to his conversation.

What just happened? Was that an aggressive maneuver? Am I being challenged? Should I claim the basket back?

The basket is too far away, actually, for me to claim it back. I'm trying to figure out what's going on, when the first course arrives. It's in a mug and I have no idea what it is.

I studied the tasting menu (which was in French) only for a brief moment, long enough to know that I wanted to order it—why not taste it all, I figured, during this once-in-a-lifetime experience?—and now I have no idea what, specifically, I have ordered.

In the mug is a layer of brown with foam on top. I take a bite and realize that it's foie gras. Ah, yes, I remember. This is a foie gras cappuccino. The foam picks up the foie gras's essence and I admire the strange alchemy of the flavors and textures.

The waitress returns to refill my water glass, and, seeing that the bread basket has moved, she moves it back so it's in front of me. She walks away and the man turns and regards me and then turns back to his female companion.

"Aha!" I cheer, in my head. "Now who possesses the bread basket? I possess it, that's who!"

But before I can declare a clear and utter victory, the

female companion gestures to the bread basket and the man slides it back over. She takes a piece from it and gives me a cool, mean look.

Hey, what did I do? I want to say. But I can't because I don't speak the language. And there I am again, without a bread basket to show for myself. A waiter takes away my eaten foie gras cappuccino and replaces it with the second course: a carpaccio, I believe, of scallop. Some kind of fish. Each sliver is coated with spices. There's pepper, there's caviar. Something briny.

"Mmmm," groans the voice in my head, finally getting more comfortable in these environs (the wine is helping). Texture is the name of the game here, as these spices are crunchy and snappy and completely different from and complementary to the smoothness of the fish.

"What are these spices?" I wonder as I chew. If I had a companion here we could talk about it.

"Is that coriander I detect?" he might say.

"No," I'd say. "I believe those are fennel seeds."

"Preposterous!"

"I dare say, you're awfully rude."

My imaginary companion is Oscar Wilde.

Companionship, I realize, is what I crave most as this meal progresses. There are times where being alone is incredibly pleasurable. There are times I love to be by myself. I love to go to museums by myself, on rainy afternoons I love to see movies by myself. I've gone to Broadway shows by myself, I've gone on rides at Disney World by myself (because my friends didn't want to wait for Peter Pan's

Flight, the fools). Solitude is not something I fear, it's something I frequently desire.

But here at this restaurant, in this strange environment where it's dark and the people look serious, I feel extraordinarily alone. I feel out of place on many levels: I don't speak the language; I'm not versed in food and wine the way many Parisians are; I'm not monied or elite; I'm not well dressed: my suit is lame and has cat hair on it.

Yet, when I really allow the solitude to sink in it suddenly becomes empowering. People don't know me here. I don't speak the language. So what do I care what anyone thinks? Let them judge me with their silent stares, I'll judge them right back. For all they know I could be a famous American writer here to document all of their antics. Actually, I am a writer here to document all of their antics. I don't need companionship: my companionship is the audience in my head—the one that will hear these stories when the meal is over. I imagine myself standing before an audience relating my experience: *What's the deal with French people and their bread baskets?* I say like Jerry Seinfeld in front of a red curtain. *What's the deal with that?*

As if on cue, the waitress returns and slides the bread basket back in my direction. Another victory!

She replaces the carpaccio with a plate that I can't parse in any way. Is it fish? Is it *brain?* I have no idea. It's covered with truffles, though, and their flavor is loud.

"My, these truffles are glorious!" I declare to my imaginary audience. "I wish you were here to try them." The

audience watches with great interest as I nibble and consider. "They taste fungal," I reveal. "And earthy. But not
unpleasant."

When I finish, the brains are removed and my wineglass
is empty.

"Another glass?" asks the waitress.

"Why, yes."

"Perhaps a red?" she suggests.

"Wonderful," I answer. "What do you suggest?"

"Medoc." She removes a wine list and points. "It won't
overpower the fish but it's strong enough for the lamb."

"Excellent."

My imaginary audience watches as I steal another piece
of bread and gloat to my bitter neighbors. The whole
bread business is so bizarre that it is, in its way, a perfect
thing to happen: a circumstance so peculiar that it flips the
tone of the evening from tragedy to comedy. Whereas before I was timid and frightened, now I am distanced and
laughing. Bread basket antics have made my experience re-
latable and surely the audience is on my side.

The waitress returns with the Medoc and the soup
course—less an actual soup and more a curious interpreta-
tion of soup: a gelatinous green layer on top of a mousse-
like brown layer. There are mushrooms mixed in and the
whole thing is creamy and luscious.

"Notice the way Robuchon plays with texture," I tell
my audience. "He makes food that is delicious but also
surprising. That's why he's so important." The audience
nods in agreement with my insight.

After the gelatinous soup, there's another unidentifiable course. I identify bacon, I identify potatoes. "Sweet, foamy, light," I declare in my head.

An audience member rises and says, "You really should pay more attention to what you ordered."

Security immediately removes him from my cranium.

Then there's lamb. And Robuchon's famous mashed potatoes.

"The secret," I tell my audience, "is an equal ratio of butter to potato."

My mother and grandmother rise up and start booing. "That's so unhealthy! You're going to have a heart attack. There's *heart disease* in your family."

"Leave him alone," says Ruth Reichl from the balcony. "Let him eat what he wants."

As reality blurs with fantasy I finally begin to understand what is miraculous about dining alone: this audience isn't real. There *is* no audience to react to your choices, to pass judgment on what you're eating. You can cater to your every whim, your every desire, without scrutiny. And the story you tell later is a story you shape yourself, one that either includes or omits significant details. The experience is yours alone.

The waitress places a small glass in front of me with tequila, chopped fruit, ices, and a fruit chip. Orange? Passion fruit? Who knows.

And then another dessert arrives. A very decadent, whipped chocolate mousse. I'm not a chocolate person especially but I dig in with abandon. Do I finish every last bite or do I show restraint and only eat half? The answer is mine to keep forever.

Soon the check arrives. It is 1 a.m. and the bill is 129 euros. That's close to $170.

"Well," I tell myself as I hand the waitress my debit card. "I've done it. I've dined alone at L'Atelier Joël Robuchon."

When I look around me, I see that I am basically by myself. The restaurant is closing up and I'm one of the last remaining. Alone, as I started, but much better off. I feel full and happy. The secret, it turns out, is a psychological one. I became the star of "The Story of My Paris Dinner" and somehow I was no longer alone: I was there with all of the people who'd be hearing this story later. I used a writerly trick: I shaped a narrative to fit this moment, a warming narrative, a comedy, one with a happy ending.

Too many people, I think, use a preexisting narrative in situations like these. *That'd be too sad,* they think when considering a meal out alone. They think of sappy Meg Ryan movies where she sits at a table by herself, sorrowful music playing, rain trickling down the window. She stirs her coffee slowly with a spoon. *No,* they think, *that won't be me. I'd rather stay in my hotel.*

And they do. They stay in their hotels and eat something fast, something easy. They want a preapproved story, one that requires all characters to dine in pairs. And they convince themselves that they're not missing much, that it's just food. But I know, my experience over now, that they are missing so much more. When you dine out alone you create an event, one that is amplified by the significance of your destination. It's one thing to eat at Bob's Big Boy by yourself, it's another to eat at Joël Robuchon. And just as with any other event that is exclusive and unique, a once-in-a-lifetime experience, it will live on forever in your memory like a precious artifact.

So as I rise from my seat, I feel the certainty that this night—despite the bread, despite my nerves, despite the cost—deserves a special display in my mental museum, to be studied and considered over the course of a lifetime. I imagine myself as an old man gazing upon the display as I'm fed Jell-O in my government discount nursing home.

The maître d' hands me my jacket and leads me to the door, opening it for me one last time.

"Good night, Monsieur Adam," he says, smiling, as I make my way out into the cool night air.

"Bonsoir," I say, smiling back. I return to the Paris night with my camera in one pocket and my Moleskine in the other, my Zadie Smith book under my arm and, protected and fussed over in the newest corridor of my brain, the Hope Diamond of dining out: the precious stone that's been this night, the night I dined in Paris alone.

TEN

Feast

You are invited to a feast.

We've reached the final chapter of the book and it's time to celebrate, and what better way to celebrate than with a feast? I'm planning an epic summer feast to commemorate the end of our book's journey.

Planning a feast is an exciting endeavor. Unlike, say, planning a dinner, where you limit yourself to an appetizer, an entrée, and a dessert, a feast requires more courses, more of everything. People must leave high on a cloud of food and wine, their vision foggy from the pink and orange sparks of gastronomical ecstasy.

My first plan is simple: I can cook a big main course and ask people to bring the other courses. I'll tell them what to bring so there's a pattern to it, a logic to the meal that one might not find at a potluck.

But that very term—*potluck*—is thrown back at me when I suggest the idea to my friends. "So this is a potluck?" they ask when I explain the concept.

"No," I say. "It's a feast."

They nod but I know they don't believe me.

"So you're cooking us a feast," says my friend James. "Except we also have to do the cooking?"

"No," I say. "I'll do most of the cooking."

But when I get home I realize that this won't do at all; I can't ask people to cook for my feast. If the purpose of this meal is to celebrate my achievement as a burgeoning gourmet, my capacity to feed others, then I actually have to feed others.

Fine, then, I decide. I'm going to cook a feast and I'm going to cook everything. This is my moment to shine, to share—in dramatic fashion—everything I've learned over the course of writing this book, everything I've learned since that very first moment when I fell in love with food.

When was that moment? I ask myself as I sit down to plan my feast. *How did all of this come about anyway? Why do I care so much about eating?*

It's five years earlier and I am in Atlanta. It's my first month of law school and life is ugly. A few months ago, my first long-term relationship ended. I am living alone in my first one-bedroom apartment and I miss my old roommates, my old college friends, my old life. My new cat (and first pet), Lolita, is sick and sleeping in my closet, sneezing from the cold she caught at the Humane Society where I adopted her.

Not only is life ugly, though, life is sad. Life is scary. *What am I doing here?* I constantly ask myself as I make my way from law-school class to law-school class. Who are these people? They are nothing like me. These are people who enjoy logic and reason and who imagine themselves as partners in a law firm one day. I can hardly imagine myself as a lawyer, let alone a partner. What am I doing here? How did I get here?

I have a vague memory of filling out law school applications, at the strong behest of my parents. Yes, I'm mostly here because my parents wanted me to be here. "You can be anything you want to be," my mom used to tell me when I was younger, "as long as you're a doctor, a lawyer, or an Indian chief." Since premed didn't work out in college (after chemistry, biology, organic chemistry, and physics), I was now in law school. Maybe I should've chosen option three.

So it's true: I'm partly here because of my parents but also slightly here because of me. I've deluded myself into thinking that I can make money as a lawyer that will support a career in the arts. By day a lawyer and by night a writer: I will go home every day and work on a novel and if that takes off I can quit my law job. That's the secret logic of my existence.

Then national tragedy strikes. When September 11 happens, I'm in contracts class and suffering through a lecture on consideration. The world seems to be falling apart and then the world literally falls apart. Like everyone else in America, I am devastated and I go home in a daze.

That night, a few friends come over and we order Chinese food. There is fear in the air because the Centers for Disease Control is just down the block and there are rumors that it too is a potential target. My mom keeps calling to check in on us, but we're okay. Just stunned, saddened, and scared. That's the timbre of the moment.

Time marches on in a haze. I go to class, type notes on my laptop, go home exhausted, and sink into my couch. The couch, like the world around me, swallows me whole. I flip on the TV and stare at the light and color and barely comprehend what I am watching.

Then, one day, buried in my couch, I discover a new thing to watch, a new channel where the colors are brighter, the sounds more varied, and the stories simple to follow. "Today we're going to make quiche," "Now we're going to make tomato sauce." It is the Food Network—the old Food Network of Sarah Moulton and Mario Batali—and day in, day out it becomes like medicine.

I come home from a soul-deadening day of civil procedure and torts and allow this strange, exotic world of food to seduce me with its promise of sensation—real sensation—not the cool, gray academic sensation of answering a question right (a rare occurrence for me), but the real, vibrant sensations that only can be offered by food. Chiles, vinegar, garlic, rosemary—these tonics of taste are precisely what's lacking from my life.

My diet, like my diet in college, consists of processed foods purchased from take-out places and supermarket frozen food aisles. The greatest thing I know how to cook, at this point, is a frozen California Pizza Kitchen pizza. Five or six boxes fill my freezer.

But now I am aware of this other planet of existence, a planet populated by passionate people, people passionate about food.

And so, one night, inspired by what I've seen on TV, I journey into my kitchen armed with groceries and a recipe. I am going to make Mario Batali's tomato sauce, the very recipe you saw at the start of this book.

I messily chop the onion. I use preminced garlic. I scrape thyme off the stems and grate a carrot. I stand over the pot as the flavors come together. I burn the garlic a little but I ignore it. I don't care. I add the tomatoes and stir softly as they give up their juices, as they give up their sweetness. The sauce reduces and I feel myself slowly come back to life. The simple act of stirring and smelling makes me feel like a real human again.

And then tasting it, along with the pasta I make (way overcooked, but I don't know any better), I feel warmed all over—as if all the cool surfaces of my heart, so thoroughly covered in frost, are beginning to melt.

This is the moment when it happens. In this moment I know that the big things that I'm worried about—my life, my career, where I'm headed—matter little as long as I can focus on something seemingly small, such as what I'm going to cook for dinner. If I can displace the lack of enthusiasm I have for the law with this newfound enthusiasm I have for food, I'll be okay. I won't cry my way through law school, I'll *cook* my way through law school.

And for the next three years, that's precisely what I do.

Food is solace, food is comfort. Recalling how important food was for me at that time in my life, I want my guests to regard this feast like a giant hug: I'll fill their bellies with so much food they'll explode with love.

Reconsidering, though, I decide that I don't want to stuff my guests until they're sick; that's a bad plan. The nineteenth-century French gastronome Brillat-Savarin wrote: "Those persons who suffer from indigestion, or who become drunk, are utterly ignorant of the true principles of eating and drinking." This feast can't be an orgy of gluttony; it must be like a work of art, it must be *designed* so that people are satisfied and full but just full enough.

I gather all of my cookbooks, all of my resources. I get out a notepad and place sticky notes in the pages of the cookbooks where I see recipes I like. On the notepad I start sketching out meal ideas.

After several days of this, and a few conversations with friends and food people (Ruth Reichl ate with me around this time, and she suggested I make as much as I can before the actual feast, otherwise I'd be too harried to enjoy it), I develop a menu:

Adam's Triumphant Summer Feast

*Heirloom Tomato Salad with Green and Purple
Basil and Fresh Feta*

Chilled Corn Soup

Leg of Lamb with Soy Garlic Marinade

Ratatouille

Goat Cheese Torta

*Strawberries and Peaches with Balsamic
Zabaglione*

I contact Derrick Schneider to help me with wine pairings. He replies with detailed information and suggestions, which I forward to my guests. They'd each have to bring a bottle of wine; there will be two of the same kind for each course. Thus we'd have ten bottles of wine for ten people, a whole bottle for each person: we're going to be an army of winos.

The next step is dealing with the lamb: where to get my leg of lamb? I call Florence Butchers, excellent butchers on Jones Street. I tell them that I want a leg of lamb that will serve ten people.

"So you want the whole leg?"

"Yes," I say.

"Do you want any bones removed?"

Do I want any bones removed? I'm not sure. I haven't chosen a specific recipe yet.

I go on eGullet, the Web community for food enthusiasts, and start a thread titled "Leg of Lamb." I write that I've never cooked a leg of lamb before, that I'm cooking for ten people, and that I don't know what to do, how to prepare it, or what to tell the butcher.

I receive many enthusiastic replies, but the most enthusiastic comes from a man who suggests I slow-cook the leg for seven hours at 150 degrees. I should have the leg end deboned but leave the shank end as is. I should make slits across the lamb and put anchovies in each slit or, alternatively, use Julia Child's marinade from her cookbook.

I decide on the latter and call the butcher with instructions on how I want my lamb deboned.

"Perfect," says the kind woman's voice. "We'll see you on Friday."

I spend the whole week before the feast on practical matters such as: Where will everyone sit? What will everyone use to eat? Will I use paper plates or will this be a grown-up meal with real plates and silverware?

The matter of seating is the most pressing concern. All I have is a cheap wooden table from Rooms to Go that seats four people. There will be ten of us. What will I do?

The roof of my building has two tables that hold eight, and that may be a solution, but this week in New York is one of the hottest on record with a heat index of 115 degrees. Eating dinner on the roof in such heat might lead to ecstasy of another sort: delirium and heatstroke. That won't do.

So I go to Bed Bath & Beyond and buy a folding table that, when set against my other table, seats ten. I also buy cheap dinner plates, dessert plates, and bowls for everyone. I know it will make a difference to eat off of something nicer than paper and, also, I can use these again. To gild the lily I buy white tablecloths and real cloth napkins. This will be a feaster's feast—I will spare no expense.

When I get home I set it all up, this being a few days before the actual feast. I have just enough drinking glasses, wineglasses, forks, knives, and spoons. I fold the napkins into triangles and set the table like a character out of *Gosford Park*. When I am done I take a step back and behold my work: the table looks good. I am well on my way.

On Thursday night I solidify my game plan. On Friday, the day before the feast, I will cook most of everything. I'll make the soup, the ratatouille, hummus to serve with the bread, the goat cheese torta from *The Babbo Cookbook,* and the marinade for the lamb. Then I'll spread the marinade over the lamb, cover it, and let it rest in the fridge overnight.

Friday morning I wake up and head straight to the farmer's market, where I'll get the ingredients for the corn soup and the ratatouille.

The corn soup has three ingredients: corn, water, and salt. Ten ears of corn serves seven, so I figure I'll buy twenty and have some soup left over.

Now I must pose a question to you, reader. Have you ever lifted twenty ears of corn? Let me tell you something: corn is heavy. It is very heavy. I purchase twenty ears of corn and suddenly I am pregnant with quadruplets, except the pregnancy is dangling from my arms and I can barely move.

But I somehow move to another vegetable stand where I buy tomatoes, zucchini, eggplant, basil, and onions for the ratatouille. By the time I am done I can't budge, so I hail a cab and return to my apartment, where I drop everything off.

Next I head to Whole Foods for the rest of the ingredients. I buy the basics: soy sauce, garlic, cream, milk, and several other things I need, such as fig jam and fresh mint for the goat cheese torta. By the time I return to my apartment it is two o'clock. I haven't even started cooking.

But I need to run out for the lamb, so I go downtown to Florence Meat Market. I hurriedly enter the store, with its sawdust on the floor and meat hanging overhead.

A smiling woman asks me if I need help and I tell her I am there to pick up a leg of lamb.

"You're Adam?"

"Yes," I say.

"Okay, one second."

She goes into the back and I begin studying the diagrams on the wall, showing various cuts of meat, including cuts from a lamb. I worry over my preparation: not only will I have to marinate it, refrigerate it, and cook it for seven hours, but various cookbooks tell me I'll have to tie it too. Tying a big piece of meat like that with kitchen string ensures even cooking. But the techniques described baffle me and I wonder if I'll be able to do it.

Just then the woman returns with a giant package wrapped in butcher paper and says, "Let me show you what we did."

She pulls back the paper and shows me the enormous leg of lamb tied expertly with butcher's string.

"We gave you an extra big one because you're feeding ten people."

She wraps it back up, puts it in a bag, and I pay her.

"How are you cooking it?"

"I'm slow-cooking it: seven hours at 150 degrees."

She gives me a strange look and says, "Like a pot roast?"

"Yes. Like a pot roast."

She nods pensively and hands me the bag. "Well, enjoy the lamb."

"Thanks for your help," I say, toting the leg-filled bag out of the store. I take a bus home, the leg of lamb resting comfortably in my lap.

The preparations begin with the corn soup. The recipe comes from *The Gourmet Cookbook*.

I pull off the husk from the first ear of corn and marvel at its shimmering, juicy kernels. This is the peak season for corn and I suddenly understand why Ruth Reichl balked at the corn at Esca: this is real corn, bursting with life. I do as Suzanne Goin recommends in *Sunday Suppers at Lucques* to see if corn is fresh: I taste a raw kernel. Summer literally explodes in my mouth and I know I am in a good place.

Then begins the labor of cutting the kernels off the cobs, which is made much easier by my supersharp knives, sharpened by the knife master at Korin. I lay a cob on its side and scrape the knife across, as recommended in *The Gourmet Cookbook*. Kernels shoot everywhere, but mostly they stay on my cutting board. I lift piles of them into my huge stockpot and continue until all twenty cobs are scraped clean.

Then I do what the recipe describes, a very simple process that I can sum up as follows: simmer the kernels with water and salt until tender; blend (I use my immersion blender), strain, and chill. That's it!

While the strained corn soup is cooling, I set about making the Barefoot Contessa's hummus. You take two cups of chickpeas (about one can), four cloves of fresh minced garlic, sesame paste, lemon juice, and the chickpea water and place them all in a food processor. Hit puree and you've got hummus! (Isn't that a Nora Ephron movie?) Scrape the hummus into a bowl, cover, and you're done.

And now it's time for the ratatouille. On my "Leg of Lamb" thread on eGullet, a chorus of commenters suggest that I serve ratatouille as my side. This works because I need something vegetarian to serve as an entrée for my vegetarians (Stella and Lisa), and ratatouille is substantial enough to be a main course.

This recipe is time consuming but well worth it. The result is aromatic, complex, and nice to look at. Plus, as is common knowledge in the ratatouille-making community, it improves overnight in the refrigerator as the flavors meld. Which is perfect for making ahead.

Ratatouille
From *The Gourmet Cookbook*

Serves 8 to 10

2 1/2 pounds tomatoes (4 large), peeled and
    coarsely chopped
8 large garlic cloves, thinly sliced
1 cup chopped fresh flat-leaf parsley
20 fresh basil leaves, torn in half
1 cup plus 2 tablespoons extra-virgin olive oil
2 1/4 teaspoons salt
2 large onions (1 1/2 pounds total), quartered
    lengthwise and thinly sliced lengthwise
3 assorted bell peppers (green, red, and/or yellow;
    1 1/2 pounds total), cored, seeded, and cut into
    1-inch-wide pieces
4 medium zucchini (2 pounds total), quartered
    lengthwise and cut crosswise into 3/4-inch-thick
    pieces

1 (2-pound) eggplant, cut into 1-inch cubes
$\frac{1}{2}$ teaspoon freshly ground black pepper

Combine tomatoes, garlic, parsley, basil, and $\frac{1}{3}$ cup oil in a 5-quart heavy pot, bring to a simmer, and simmer, covered, stirring occasionally, until tomatoes break down and sauce is slightly thickened, about 30 minutes.

Meanwhile, heat 3 tablespoons oil in a 12-inch heavy skillet over moderate heat. Add onions with $\frac{1}{4}$ teaspoon salt and cook, stirring occasionally, until softened, 10 to 12 minutes. With a slotted spoon, transfer onions to a large bowl. Add 3 more tablespoons oil to skillet and cook bell peppers, with $\frac{1}{4}$ teaspoon salt, stirring occasionally, until softened, about 10 minutes. With slotted spoon, transfer peppers to bowl with onions. Add 3 more tablespoons oil to skillet and cook zucchini, with $\frac{1}{4}$ teaspoon salt, stirring occasionally, until softened, 8 to 10 minutes. With slotted spoon, transfer zucchini to bowl with other vegetables. While zucchini is cooking, pat eggplant dry with paper towels. Add remaining oil (scant $\frac{1}{4}$ cup) to skillet and cook eggplant over moderate heat, stirring occasionally, until softened, 10 to 12 minutes.

Add vegetables, remaining salt, and pepper to tomato sauce and simmer, covered, stirring occasionally, until vegetables are very tender, about 1 hour.

Season ratatouille with salt. Cool, uncovered, and serve warm or at room temperature.

Note: The ratatouille can be made up to 2 days ahead and refrigerated, covered. Bring to room temperature or reheat, if desired.

It is midnight and I am getting weary. I will have to be up early the next morning to meet Diana and Stella to go shopping for the rest of our necessities: bread from Amy's Bread, antipasto from Murray's Cheese, and then fresh tomatoes, peaches, and strawberries from the farmer's market.

The final two things that I need to do, though, go fairly quickly. The first is the bizarre goat cheese torta I stumbled upon in *The Babbo Cookbook*. This, I thought when I read it, could be a perfect cheese course, marking the transition from savory to sweet with a dazzling mix of flavors. It requires two pounds of goat cheese, preferably Coach Farm. I've enjoyed Coach Farm in the past but at Whole Foods, where I buy the ingredients, the Coach Farm goat cheese is five dollars for a quarter pound. Do the math and you realize that will be forty dollars for the dish, too much in the larger context of how much I'm spending.

So I buy a more conventional goat cheese (which works fine) and begin the strange process of making this dish: layering goat cheese between liquid layers of basil pesto and fig jam (the secret, I realize, is to flatten the goat cheese like a pancake in my hand first and then to simply lay it on top). Finally, I get to the lamb, which is waiting patiently in the refrigerator.

Julia Child's marinade (from *Mastering the Art of French Cooking*) is simple and logical in that these flavors, quite clearly, are ones that you would want to permeate your lamb overnight. Here's what you do: blend ½ cup Dijon mustard, 2 tablespoons soy sauce, 1 clove mashed garlic, 1 teaspoon ground rosemary or thyme, and ¼ teaspoon powdered ginger. Then drizzle in olive oil as you stir to make a mayonnaise-like cream. I double the recipe because my lamb leg is so big. I rub it all over the lamb, place it on the rack of my roasting pan, cover with aluminum foil, and place it in my fridge overnight.

And then, with the exhaustion and excitement of a bride the night before her wedding day, I go to bed. Twenty-four hours later we will be feasting.

I sleep fitfully, waking throughout the night worried over some detail that I've forgotten. Will the lamb really cook at such a low temperature? Will people really be full enough from what I make? Will they really enjoy themselves?

At seven-fifteen I awake, shower and dress, and make my way down to Amy's Bread in the Village. Craig comes along with me and we meet Stella and Diana there to begin our morning shopping.

This is the enchanted hour, New York in the morning, the city still asleep with only a few purposeful souls like us gallivanting around. At Amy's Bread, Stella sips coffee; Diana is still on her way.

I speak to the woman behind the counter, who wears a bandana on her head and appears quite alert for such an early hour.

"I'm having a dinner party tonight," I say. "There will be ten of us. How much bread do I need?"

"About two or three loaves," she suggests.

I study the shelves and see what I want. "Raisin fennel for sure," I say and I watch her pull it off the shelf.

"Then I guess we want something plain," I continue. "The French loaf?"

"That's good. Do you want it sliced?"

"Yes," I say. Over my shoulder, Stella and Craig sit at a table, looking glazed over.

"That should be enough," I conclude, and then I spy the olive bread. "Oh. The olive bread looks good too."

"You want it?"

"Okay." This is a feast after all.

After I pay, the three of us move next door to Murray's Cheese, a Village staple, and Diana staggers in late. She, Stella, and Craig watch as I approach the counter.

"How can I help you?" a young woman asks.

"I'm having a feast tonight," I say. "And we need some stuff for an antipasto platter."

In front of me are various tins of traditional antipasto food, so I know I am standing in the right spot.

"My favorite thing here are the Peppadews," she says. "They're spicy and sweet. Here, try one."

She hands me one and I bite into this red, juicy, spicy pepper and feel my mouth heat up. This is a strange thing to eat at eight in the morning.

"I like it. We need enough for ten people."

I watch her fill a tub and then I spy precut artichokes and ask for a few of those. This antipasto course, the people arriving course, will be served with Prosecco—a sparkling Italian wine that is one of the few things you can pair with artichokes, otherwise a bad combination with wine.

We continue with stuffed grape leaves, small mozzarella balls, and finally sliced meat: soppresatta.

From Murray's we head to the farmer's market to stock up on the final necessities. First: strawberries. At a sunlit table staffed by three men, people stand in line for tubs of wild strawberries stacked in a cardboard box. Since this is the only line at the market this morning, I take it as evidence of something special (something that "looks good," as I learned in chapter 2), so I get in line.

"These must be special berries," I tell Stella and Diana. "Otherwise why would people line up like this?"

As I get closer to the front of the line I see the strawberries in the box whittle away. By the time I get to the front the last strawberries have been purchased.

I almost yelp out, "But aren't there any more? I'm having a feast!"

And just then one of the three men reaches under the table and pulls out another cardboard crate of strawberries.

"Phew," I say to myself and when he asks me how many I want I say three. I only *need* two, but these are special and tonight is a special night.

Then, Stella and Diana join me as I pick six fresh peaches (which I later realize aren't ripe) and then, finally, heirloom tomatoes from an enthusiastic tomato lady.

"You must be having a tomato party," she says, seeing how many tomatoes I am buying.

We select the most freakishly shaped heirloom tomatoes we can find. The woman is so particular in helping me that the people behind me in line are tutting their tongues in irritation. "Sorry," she tells them. "This young man is having a tomato party. I'm helping him."

Tomatoes selected, and green and purple basil purchased from a final vendor, Stella, Diana, and I lift our bags with contentment and walk northward to my apartment. Our shopping is done and the final preparations begin.

The lamb goes in the oven at noon. We brown it first at 400 degrees, as the recipe writer suggests. Then we take it out of the oven, lower the temperature to 150 (my oven protests, stopping at 170), and place it back in, inserting a probe thermometer into its middle and setting the timer on it for seven hours.

"So it begins," I say as I close the oven door.

Next, we set to making balsamic zabaglione, also from *The Babbo Cookbook*. This will be served with the peaches and strawberries after coating them in a honey vin santo glaze (vin santo is a sweet Italian dessert wine). The process requires serious whisking and Diana's strong wrist is a significant contribution to our cause.

We do the peach and strawberry glaze after finishing the zabaglione (which we refrigerate), and pour it on the cut peaches and strawberries, which we know will make them release their juices, but we decide this is better done now than during the feast. We set the bowl above the refrigerator and begin our final endeavor, the tomatoes.

The tomatoes are fun to cut. Stella cuts out the dirty patches (these are heirlooms, with weird grooves and scars) and I cut them up, the small ones into wedges and the large ones into slices.

They all go into a pretty blue bowl awaiting further treatment. I decide I won't dress them until we get to the tomato course, otherwise they will release too much juice.

With the bowl of tomatoes complete, Stella, Diana, and I realize that we are done. Diana runs out to get her wine, Stella sets to tidying, and I go to shower, wanting to look spiffy for the first guest.

These final moments are the pleasant, heart-pleasing ones that happen before any major event. It's the feeling before a party, before a ceremony, before graduation. The buzz of excitement that makes your life feel festive and happy, the buzz of excitement that happens so rarely as we grow older.

This is a happy time, I realize. A happy time that's been a long time coming.

• • •

How did I get from the spiritual starvation of law school to the land of abundance where I am now? Was food merely a distraction or was food something more? Did food save me or did I save myself?

I cooked my way through law school. After watching Sarah Moulton do it on her show, I made fried zucchini with kalamata olive dipping sauce; I made a Mario Batali pasta dish with garlic and anchovies that thoroughly stank up my apartment. I even attempted making steak.

The summer after my first year I moved in with Lauren (whom you met in the first chapter) and began enacting more cooking experiments in our shared kitchen: lasagna from the French Laundry cookbook; sponge cake with berries and whipped cream; Jacques Torres's chocolate mudslide cookies.

When the next school year started, I was much less depressed because cooking for myself gave me an occupation outside of my law school existence. I discovered food magazines *(Gourmet, Saveur),* I bought more and more cookbooks, and I stayed up late to watch Martha Stewart when her show was mostly helpful cooking tips.

The next summer, I scored a job working for a law firm in L.A. The work there—assembling cardboard boxes, delivering papers to courthouses—left me deeply unfulfilled, but outside the firm I blossomed as a lover of food. I read my first food book, *Feeding a Yen,* by Calvin Trillin.

Calvin Trillin led me to Chowhound, the insider foodie Web site, and Chowhound led me to Jonathan Gold, whose book *Counter Intelligence* is essential for anyone living in Los Angeles who cares about food.

Counter Intelligence became my life. I began going on food adventures every day after work. I went to Silver Lake for the best Cuban sandwich, I drove thirty miles north for the best pizza. My college friend J.C., who lived in L.A. at the time, came with me once to an obscure burger stand literally in the middle of nowhere. We thought twice before getting out of the car.

"Are you sure this place is legit?"

"I'm sure," I assured him.

The burger there (a chili burger) was tasty, as was almost all the other food I discovered that summer: perfect roast chicken at Zankou Chicken (served with their mysterious, incredibly potent white garlic sauce), wildly fresh Mexican food at Loteria in the farmer's market, and world-class burgers and fries at In-N-Out Burger.

Surprisingly, my fellow interns at the law firm also shared an interest in food, or, more likely, in the opportunity to leave the office for extended periods of time. As a group we ate the classic French dip sandwich at Philippe's (where, apparently, the French dip was invented), scarfed scallop burritos at Señor Fish, and devoured New York–rivaling pastrami at Langer's. I ate well in Los Angeles.

When I got back to Atlanta, I decided that class-action lawsuits weren't really my thing and that I might be happier doing public-interest law. So I signed up for work at the Atlanta Legal Aid AIDS project, where I assisted attorneys in preparing wills and living wills for HIV and AIDS patients around Atlanta.

I immediately felt good about where I was. I liked the work I was doing, but what I liked even better was cooking for my coworkers. My food life was in high gear: I was cooking and baking at a regular clip. I loved baking the best: it was the most consistently rewarding. Follow the instructions, take your time with all the steps, and out comes sweet, buttery perfection. I rewarded all of my coworkers with zingy lemon bars, intense chocolate brownies, and deeply comforting homemade chocolate chip cookies.

I took their enthusiastic consumption of these baked goods as a sign that they were appreciated. And I took for granted that the legal work I was doing was good. They asked me to research a legal issue, I went on Lexis-Nexis and typed in the keywords, printed out a few articles and cases, handed them in, and patted myself on the back.

And then there was a rude awakening. I received my midsemester evaluation and it was a *bad* one. They gave me a C-minus and said my research skills were "that of a first-year, not a third-year, law student." But what about my cookies? What about my lemon bars?

I went to talk to the "boss," or the figurehead in the office, John Warchol, whose office was directly parallel to my desk. I couldn't help but feel deeply wounded.

I trusted John and I really respected him. Who wouldn't

respect someone who devotes his entire life to helping the sick and helpless for teensy amounts of money? I considered him a saint and he'd given me a C-minus.

"Adam," he said after I sat in the chair opposite him, "I'm going to say something now that you may not want to hear."

"What?"

He took a moment and then leaned forward on his desk. "Your heart isn't in this," he said.

The clarity of his statement was jarring.

"Why do you want to be a lawyer?"

"Well," I said, "I like helping people. And I like reading and writing, and law involves that."

He gave me a look that said more than words might. "I just don't understand why you're doing this," he said, finally. "It's just clear to all of us that the law isn't for you."

I went home that night and worried myself to sleep. *Who does he think he is telling me the law isn't for me? I do decent work. No one's said anything like this before.*

The next morning, however, when I woke up, I did something unexpected. I printed out a play I wrote over the summer and I read it. It'd been a few months since I'd looked at it, and I realized that it was good. It was lively and funny and unique. I could do something with it.

So I revised it and printed out three applications to grad schools in dramatic writing: one to Yale, one to Juilliard, and one to NYU/Tisch.

A few days later, I did something else. My friends Josh and Katy had urged me to start a food blog. I'd been posting on food forums like Chowhound and eGullet for a while. After my review of Charlie Trotter's caused a frenzied debate and a defense of my position from Anthony Bourdain, I knew that Josh and Katy were on to something.

So I started my blog, "The Amateur Gourmet," in January 2004, right after my legal aid internship ended. I began by making Martha Stewart pecan chocolate chip cookies, writing about weird fruit I found at Whole Foods, and reviewing a few restaurants that I frequented.

Then, somewhat notoriously, Janet Jackson showed her breast at the Superbowl and as a joke, I made a Janet Jackson breast cupcake. I posted it on my site at 11 p.m. a few days after the incident. I went to bed, got up, went to school, and when I came home I was astounded at what I found when I turned on my computer.

My site had received 100,000 hits just that morning (up to that point it was twenty or thirty hits a day). The post was linked all over the Web, from collegehumor.com to instapundit. I had more than a hundred e-mails in my inbox and one of them was from CNN: they wanted to come over to shoot a segment.

And then, a few months later, it came: a small envelope that probably spelled rejection. I'd received one from Yale a week earlier, got another from Juilliard after that, and this one from NYU looked no different. But I opened it there, standing in front of my mailbox, and felt my blood tingle and my skin electrify as I read the word on the paper when I pulled it out.

"Congratulations." I had been accepted to NYU's graduate program in dramatic writing. Instantly I saw a new future for myself, a future in New York, a future that made me profoundly happy. I would start a new life, meet new people, and craft a career that would fit far better than one in the law ever could.

And, once again, that's precisely what I did.

So what better, more appropriate way to end my book, than to have a magnificent celebration for these friends I've made when I put my life on the right path, when I finally realized what I wanted and did everything I could to get what I wanted before it was too late?

For that, I believe, is the link between good living and good eating that I've explored in this book. Metaphorically, food is sustenance, it is pleasure, it is the very thing we need to survive but also to live well. What happens when you order the wrong thing at a restaurant? When the food they bring out is not what you wanted, not even close? When you realize you're actually in the wrong restaurant? You either eat what you're fed, like an obedient child, or you rise up from the table and say, "I'm sorry, this isn't for me" and move on to something that is for you. That's what it means to eat like a grown-up: to know what you're hungry for and to feed yourself well.

It's not a coincidence that my food awakening coincided with my personal life awakening. In both cases I was listening to a voice deep inside, one that didn't speak of *shoulds* and *musts,* but one that spoke of hunger. And now that I've finally listened to that voice I can use it to feed others. When you are able to do that—and it can take a mighty long time to hear that voice—what better way to express your gratitude, your achievement, and to celebrate the plentitude of your spiritual life than to cook a big meal for the people you love? To feast is to relish, to gorge on the goodness that life has to offer. Have you been hungry too long? There's a feast waiting and the doorbell is ringing.

First comes Lisa, then James, then Craig and John and Ricky and Patty. Patty's girlfriend, Lauren, who is one of the ten, is sick and can't make it. We miss her but we're hungry and we sit down, eager to begin.

We start with Prosecco (an Italian sparkling wine), the antipasto, and the bread. We sit around the table, the sun beating through the window, and chat lightly. Music plays from speakers airported from my computer in the other room. The lamb, which is in the oven, gives off a pleasant scent. I monitor the temperature carefully.

Then, after twenty or thirty minutes of Prosecco and appetizers, it is time for the salad.

Patty is our sommelier and moves us on to the rosé that Derrick recommended. I go into the kitchen with a stack of nine small plates and layer each one with a fair amount of tomatoes. Then I tuck green and purple basil between the tomatoes. A few pieces of sliced red onion go on top, then a sprinkling of feta. Finally, I drizzle olive oil over each

plate, a few syrupy drops of good balsamic, and a sprinkling of sea salt. The plates are works of art and I present
them to my guests with raw enthusiasm.

Meanwhile, the internal temperature of the lamb is
static at 104 degrees. Strange, but I don't worry.

The guests eat their tomatoes with the rosé and the chatting continues. I feel relaxed and comfortable, capable of enjoying myself while running things. When the tomato course
is over, all of us are slightly buzzed from the two glasses of
wine. I collect the small plates and put them into the sink.

I gather everyone's bowls and remove the stockpot of
chilled corn soup from the refrigerator. I ladle the soup
into each bowl and top with chives that Diana chopped.

I serve the guests and Patty pours a Chardonnay.

"Mmmm," they remark. "It tastes so fresh."

"It's just corn, water, and salt," I declare.

"Wow," they say as they set to slurping.

Now I go to the kitchen, preparing for the main event,
and I am horrified to discover that the lamb is still at 104
degrees, not nearly the temperature it needs to be done
(135 degrees).

I open the oven door and feel inside. It is room temperature, not even remotely hot. I can put my hand on the
metal rack and it doesn't hurt. At all. This 150-degree business for seven hours is a disaster.

So I immediately spring into action, shooting the temperature up to 350 and informing my guests that the lamb
might be a little while.

They don't care—they are buzzed and happy, talking

and clinking and drinking and buttering their Amy's bread with abandon.

Rather quickly, the internal temperature of the lamb rises and before I know it we are at 135 degrees. Out of the oven it comes and I remove the lamb to a cutting board, where I let it rest.

I use the eGullet writer's recipe for gravy. I had Diana buy an extra bottle of red and I dump the entire bottle, to Diana's horror, into the roasting pan. I turn the heat up on high and let the wine boil down.

"That smells awesome," says James.

The guests are milling around my apartment at this point, needing a stretch after the first few serious rounds.

Once the wine reduces I add cream, off the heat, whisk it around, and put it back on the heat to boil down more.

After it has boiled for a while, I strain it into a bowl. The lamb, sufficiently rested, is ready to carve.

I carve off the tiniest bit from the end, nervous about how it all turned out. But the taste is extraordinary: pungent, fatty, and slightly crisp on the outside. Perfection.

I slice big pieces, lift the lid off the room-temperature ratatouille, and began dishing out plates. At this point, my actions all fall together into a kind of blur. Guests enter the kitchen carving themselves more lamb, Patty pours us red wine (a Rhone, at Derrick's suggestion, who wrote in his e-mail: "Rhone! Rhone! Rhone!"), and people praise the ratatouille ("What's in here?" they ask).

By the end of this course, we are all dizzy with food and wine and we need a break. So we go up to the roof.

• • •

The sun is setting over Manhattan and all of us grip the rail so we can lean forward and soak it all in. It is a stunning sunset, the colors rich with pink and orange, the Hudson sparkling underneath it, boats flitting past.

There is a moment of quiet reverie as each of us reflects on the night, the climate (cooler than we'd expected), and how harmonious it all is: the food, the wine, the sky, the colors, the sounds, the smells, the company.

Soon we'll all descend the stairs again and take our seats at the table. I'll serve the goat cheese torta ("This is good," says James, scraping his plate clean. "I would make this at home.") with a sparkling sweet wine (Moscato d'Asti) that has the guests cheering.

And for the final act, I'll spoon the marinated peaches and strawberries into each wineglass, topping with the zabaglione to the delight of these full, drunken feast-goers.

But up here on the roof, in the middle of it all, I know this is a crowning moment. The night sky illuminated above me, I feel like the roof is a platform, lifting me closer and closer to the constellations. I don't know my place in the firmament yet, but I know my course is a good one.

It doesn't matter where I'm going, I think as the night grows cooler and darker. I don't know what life has in store, what struggles and traumas may lay in wait, what achievements and delights the world may promise. But I know this much: I can feed myself and I can feed others, and because of that I will always, at the very least, know how to eat well.

To eat well is to live well, I have learned at the end of this book's journey. I am on my roof surrounded by people I love, with good food in our bellies and more to come, and wine buzzing our heads. My appetite is still intact, I'm ready for the food downstairs, and yet—in a funny way, a way that makes me feel less like an amateur than ever before—I have never been more full.

Do the Dishes

When I moved from Atlanta to New York, I was shocked to find that my New York apartment didn't have a garbage disposal. How could I cook if I couldn't grind my eggshells in the sink? If I had to dispose of everything in the trash?

But I adapted and survived and then I moved to Brooklyn where, unlike my Manhattan apartment, the new apartment didn't have a dishwasher.

"There's no dishwasher!" I said in shock to Diana and Craig when surveying the apartment.

"Don't worry," they said. "You'll get used to it."

Get used to it? In my old apartment, glasses, plates, cups, saucers could all go in the dishwasher at the flick of a wrist and I'd be done cleaning. I could go watch important foreign films on my DVD player or read classic works of literature. My precious time would never be wasted; the time others might spend doing dishes I'd spend cultivating a worldly persona.

But here in Brooklyn I do the dishes by hand. When I cook for Craig or Diana they usually repay me by doing the dishes for me, but often I'm standing there alone and scrubbing away mindlessly.

Mindlessly, but mindfully too. I take care with each dish: scrubbing away the gristle with the dish brush I bought from the Container Store. It fills with soap and I squirt the soap generously all over the plates and saucers and cups before I begin my scrubbing. Once I cracked a wineglass by scrubbing too hard; now I'm careful.

Doing dishes is the dreaded consequence of cooking, the dark cloud looming after a sunny day at the beach. When I first started cooking, dishes would pile up in the sink and it'd take days for me to get to them. Sometimes I'd wait so long that a batter or sauce would calcify and I'd have to throw out a plate. Now I'm better about cleaning right after cooking.

Cleaning after cooking is like showering after exercise: it's a restoration process. Exercise makes you sweaty, showering makes you clean. Same with dishes: cooking makes them dirty, cleaning restores them.

That seems obvious, but most people don't think about doing dishes in a positive way. It's like putting away your toys or picking up tennis balls after a three-hour game. It's a chore, a task, a punishment. Rich people get rich so they don't have to do their dishes. (They get richer so they don't have to cook.)

But I'm going to let you in on a secret, before we put this book to bed: doing dishes is a reward in itself.

It's an unpalatable truth, one that most won't believe. I know Diana and Craig will read that last paragraph and say, "Well, if you feel that way, you can do the dishes from here on in!"

I'm not trying to say that doing dishes is fun or exciting or stimulating. I'm simply saying that it's rewarding. If you can find reward in doing dishes, you've arrived at a happy place.

Think of it this way: it's one thing to enjoy making a mess, it's another to enjoy cleaning it up. And the sooner you embrace the cleaning up, the more likely you are to make more messes. In other words, the moment you find doing dishes rewarding is the moment you become a cook for life.

So here's my advice. When you're done with a big dinner—and as you mature with your cooking you'll find yourself preparing more and more dinners for eager and hungry friends—send everyone home with a pat on the back and an assurance that, "No, I can do the dishes, it'll be fine."

Once the door closes, stand in the kitchen and survey the scene. It'll scare you. How can so few people make such a big mess?

Turn on some music. Take off your shoes (or were they already off?). Begin with the plates: scrape the uneaten food into the trash. Stack them on the side of the sink and then gather all the cups and glasses and smaller plates and put them close by. Take the cooking vessels—the pots, the pans, the roasting pans—and see what's left. Any food for leftovers? Put it into plastic containers and refrigerate only after stealing a bite for yourself.

Now turn on the water. Get it hot—not so hot that it burns you, but hot enough that it'll do a lot of the work for you. (Hot water melts many things that would otherwise be difficult to scrub away.) Get the drying rack out and put it on a dish towel. Now take the first plate and place it under the water, squirt with soap, and start scrubbing.

If a bit of food is sticking to the plate, use your finger to peel it off. Then scrub again, rinse, and place it in the drying rack. Do this with the rest of the plates, then move on to the saucers, the cups, the glasses, and then finally the big vessels. Are you suffering through this or has your mind entered a blissful quiet place? It has? Okay, shhhh, I won't disturb you.

I'll leave you there in that quiet place, which is where I wanted to get you to anyway. It's the place that most people never have time for, a place of true tranquillity, hope, and peace. When you leave that place, you'll have a clean kitchen. And a clean kitchen is just begging to be dirtied again.

May your kitchen, then, always be somewhere between clean and dirty—in transit between the two, always in motion, never still. I wish you ovens full of sizzling succulence and sinkfuls of soaking saucers. I hope your fridge is bursting with butter, your cabinets are spilling with flour and sugar, and that your trashbags are ripe from yesterday's fish. Mostly, though, I pray that your kitchen becomes a lively place. May you never sacrifice liveliness for fear of doing dishes.

Happy cooking.

A Final Recipe

You may remember from the introduction that this is the recipe I've never been able to conquer. Perhaps now that you've finished the book, you're ready to try your hand. If you succeed, please e-mail me at amateurgourmet@ gmail.com and tell me how you did it. I need the encouragement.

Nancy Silverton's Spiced Caramel Corn

Yield: 8 servings

1 cup (4 ounces) whole macadamia nuts (optional)
$1/2$ teaspoon vegetable oil
$1/3$ cup unpopped popcorn
$1/4$ cup water

2 cups sugar

2 tablespoons light corn syrup

1 vanilla bean

³/₄ teaspoon ground cinnamon

1¹/₂ teaspoons freshly grated nutmeg

¹/₈ teaspoon ground cloves

¹/₄ teaspoon ground cardamom

1¹/₂ teaspoons kosher salt

TO TOAST THE NUTS: Preheat the oven to 325 degrees. Spread the macadamia nuts on a baking sheet, and toast them in the oven for about 10–15 minutes, until they're lightly browned. Allow the nuts to cool, and coarsely chop them in half.

TO POP THE CORN: In a medium-size pot, heat the oil over high heat. Add the popcorn and cover with a lid. Once the corn begins to pop, shake the pan constantly. When the corn has finished popping, remove from the heat and take off the lid.

In a large deep pot, at least 12 inches wide, stir together the water, sugar, and corn syrup. Using a small paring knife, split the vanilla bean in half lengthwise. With the back of the knife, scrape out the pulp and the seeds, and add the scrapings and the pod to the mixture. Stir in the cinnamon, nutmeg, cloves, cardamom, and salt. Using a pastry brush dippd in water, brush down the sides of the pan to remove any undissolved sugar granules.

Continue cooking over medium heat about 4 or 5 minutes, tilting and swirling the pan, until the mixture just begins to smoke and is a deep caramel color. Stir in the popcorn and nuts, and continue to stir until the popcorn is completely coated, moving the skillet on and off the heat to prevent the caramel from burning. Cook the mixture until it turns a deep mahogany color. Pour it onto a nonstick mat or parchment-lined baking sheet, and spread it out to cool. Remove and discard the vanilla bean.

It can be stored for up to 3 days in an airtight container.

Acknowledgments

To my parents for their incredible generosity. To Michael and Tali for their patience; to Grandma and Grandpa for being funny. ("It's just one dinner," Grandma says now when I stress over a meal.) To Lauren for being there at the start; to Lisa for sticking to her guns; to Stella, Patty, Diana, Kirk, James, and everyone else who was game for this book. To the pros who helped me: Amanda Hesser, Ruth Reichl, Eric "Bubba" Gabrynowycz, the knife master at Korin. To Liz Diggs for e-mailing Ruth; to Molly Smith Metzler for talking to Bubba; to Derrick Schneider for the wine pairings; to Jonathan Rubinstein and the people at Joe for letting me write a book in their coffee shop; to Emily Jenkins for introducing me to my agent, and, most definitely, to my agent, Elizabeth Kaplan, for discovering me, nurturing me, and championing me to the world. A big thanks to Josh and Katy for urging me to start a blog—it's really paid off! To John Warchol for changing my life with one line. And, last but not least, to my editor, Philip Rappaport, for his enthusiasm and intelligence and for getting me through my first book. I've loved every second.

Works Cited

Batali, Mario. *The Babbo Cookbook*. New York: Clarkson Potter, 2002.

Bertolli, Paul, and Alice Waters. *The Chez Panisse Cookbook*. New York: Random House, 1988.

Chang, Jae-Ok. *Vignettes of Korean Cooking*. Daegu: Maeilwensaek Press, 2000.

Child, Julia. *Mastering the Art of French Cooking*. New York: Knopf, 1961.

Garten, Ina. *Barefoot in Paris*. New York: Clarkson Potter, 2004.

Garten, Ina. *The Barefoot Contessa Cookbook*. New York: Clarkson Potter, 1999.

Garten, Ina. *The Barefoot Contessa Parties*. New York: Clarkson Potter, 2001.

Gray, Rose, and Ruth Rogers. *Italian Easy (Recipes from the London River Café)*. New York: Clarkson Potter, 2004.

Mavromataki, Maria. *The Best Traditional Recipes of Greek Cooking*. Athens: Editions Haitalis, 2002.

Nathan, Joan. *Jewish Cooking in America*. New York: Knopf, 1998.

Reichl, Ruth. *The Gourmet Cookbook*. New York: Houghton Mifflin, 2004.

Shere, Lindsey R. *Chez Panisse Desserts*. New York: Random House, 1985.

Silverton, Nancy. *Nancy Silverton's Sandwich Book*. New York: Knopf, 2002.